CHEIRO: Prophet of the End Times

Anthony Carr

Acknowledgements
I want to thank the following people: Countess Mena Hamon for her unstinting flow of material about her late husband Count Louis Hamon (Cheiro), world renowned palmist Mir Bashir, Silent Screen legend Lillian Gish, my mother Josephine Lonsdale for her continued support throughout this project, my typist Sharon MacKinnon, Niall Reid, Topaz Amber Dawn, Allen Spraggett, my longtime fellow traveler and mentor and my editor, Ian Connerty.

Dedicated to Daisy Elizabeth Stuart.

Cover Design by Lisa Carey

ISBN 0-9732222-0-4

Carr, Anthony
    Cheiro: Prophet of the End Times

Published by
Carrino Publishing, 11 Sutherland Avenue, Toronto, Canada M4C 1R8

Printed and bound by University of Toronto Press Inc.

Cheiro's prophecies made in 1925

More than 75 years ago, Cheiro looked into the future of the world and foresaw many events that have since occurred and many other events that still lie ahead. Most of these predictions were published in *World Predictions* in 1927.

Some of his visions that have come true include:
- World War II
- London and other big cities will be nearly destroyed in WW II
- Italy will annex Libya
- A new Jewish state will be recognized by the world
- The British Empire will collapse
- Britain will give up India
- Religious wars will tear India apart
- Britain will have three crowned heads of state in 25 years
- King Edward VIII will give up his throne for the love of a woman
- King George VI will leave the throne for health reasons
- His daughter, Elizabeth II, will become Queen of England
- Civil war between Northern and Southern Ireland will inflict damage in Manchester and other British cities
- There will be a revolution in the role of women in society

Prophecies for the future:
- A great era lies ahead for the United States and Britain
- A woman will be President of the United States
- Prince Charles may become King of both England and France
- Britain will face another onslaught by a foreign power
- Worldwide strife, upheaval, and revolutions
- Worldwide volcanic eruptions, earthquakes, floods, plagues and climate changes
- A worldwide religious revival
- The lost continent of Atlantis will rise in the Azores
- The Arctic will become warmer and the ice caps will melt
- Northern Europe becomes too cold to live in
- Africa, including the Sahara, becomes more temperate
- Millions migrate south into the Mediterranean countries
- World War III is centered on Palestine between 1999 and 2027
- WW III will destroy ancient cities and spread to the United States
- Immense new mineral deposits of untold wealth will be found in Palestine
- Palestine will become a new industrial center
- Russia will invade Palestine
- Russia will dominate the world for 100 years
- China is ravaged be dissent over communism
- Japan is affected by China's troubles
- Subversives cause widespread unrest in South America

CONTENTS

Anthony Carr

About Anthony Carr
The World's "*Most Documented Psychic*" ™

Anthony Carr is the author of two internationally syndicated columns: *Stargazing* and *Hands of Destiny*; three books: *Palmistry: The Hands of Destiny*, *Cheiro: Prophet of the End Times* and *Fool's Journey*, an autobiography. His predictions are also published regularly in *The National Enquirer* and the *Globe*. Carr has been called "the seer without peer," and "the world's most documented psychic" who can predict the future with such uncanny accuracy that he has been hailed as a modern day Nostradamus, especially in light of his recent prophecies concerning Princess Diana's death and the terrorist attacks on New York and Washington.

Carr first saw the light of day on December 6, 1943, under the big top, the glitzy showbiz world of circus life where his parents performed as high platform divers with Patty Conklin's world-famous *Conklin Shows* (later Conklin/American Shows), featuring Alfie Phillips' *Water Follies*. Anthony's father was billed as Captain Tony Carr, and was a former Hollywood stuntman and close friend of late 1940's movie tough guy, George Raft and real life tough guy, Benjamin *Bugsy* Siegal. Carr Sr. also worked with Billy Rose, the celebrated New York promoter of the 1930's, and MGM swimming superstar Esther Williams. Since circus folk made little money in those days, Carr grew up in a poor section of Toronto, Canada. Out of a sense that he was destined for something extraordinary and through sheer will power, he clawed his way out of grinding poverty to hob-knob with the famous and the infamous. It wasn't until later in life that Carr realized his psychic ability was something quite rare, an endowment he traces back to his Mohawk roots.

Combining palmist studies and his psychic ability, Carr began using his gift to help people. When he wasn't traveling the fair ground circuit, he continued living in the same rough neighborhood and as a young man he became street wise in order to survive. He honed his survival skills by earning a brown belt in Judo at the age of sixteen. This led to an interest in bodybuilding, and within four years he captured the title of Mr. Canada.

He then set himself the task of becoming a musician, practicing tenor saxophone for six to eight hours a day. Carr gained a reputation as one of the Canada's leading rhythm and blues musicians, working with such notables as Ronnie Hawkins and Ben E. King (of *Stand by Me* fame) before touring with his own band. This brought him into contact with many celebrities in New York, Los Angeles, London, Toronto and elsewhere. He read their palms and demonstrated his psychic abilities to the amazement of all.

Many politicians, royalty, Hollywood stars and media people know that Carr is in a class all by himself. He has done readings for Sylvester Stallone, Frank Sinatra, Glenda Jackson, Ella Fitzgerald, Lillian Gish, Richard Burton, Liberace, Cab Calloway, Peggy Lee, Mikail Gorbachev, Queen Julianna of the Netherlands, Lady Iris Mountbatten, Countess DeSalaga (descendant of Vlad the Impaler — Dracula) — and many others. He has also appeared on National TV shows hosted by Howard Stern, Phil Donahue, Roseanne Barr and others. A list of Anthony Carr's accurately fulfilled, documented predictions is at the end of this book.

Allen Spraggett is a well-known author on the paranormal. His fifteen books include *The Psychic Mafia, Arthur Ford: The man who talked with the Dead, The World of the Unexplained, The Bishop Pike Story* and *Kathryn Kuhlman: The Woman who Believes in Miracles.* Spraggett also hosted the TV show *Beyond Reason.*

Introduction

We are in the End Times. The signs are all around us: war, earthquakes, new diseases, and climate changes. These are the visions I have been having for years since I discovered my psychic gifts. Many people have called me "Dr. Doom" because of my ability to foresee airplane accidents, earthquakes and horrible events like the tragedy of the terrorist attack on the World Trade Centre in New York City on 9, 11, 2001. Many other psychics have also foreseen the End Times. Among them are Edgar Cayce and Gordon Michael Scallion. But the person who saw these events with uncanny accuracy before any of the others was the man know as Cheiro, a brilliant psychic I call the Prophet of the End Times.

This is the incredible story of Count Louis Hamon, known the world over as Cheiro. During his peak years, between 1890 and 1936, he was revered as the greatest palmist and clairvoyant since the days of Nostradamus. Born near Dublin, Ireland as William John Warner, in 1866, he was destined to become a confidant and trusted advisor to many historical figures. Cheiro or "the Count" as his friends called him, was present at some of the most important events of his time. In some of these events he would play a key role.

People still living, who visited Cheiro, say there wasn't another psychic who came close to him. For more than 25 years, he dazzled the world with his amazing powers of palmistry and clairvoyance, which enabled him to peer uncannily into the future. As a psychic palmist, none was his equal. His is a story of real ghosts and true cases of psychokinesis; about people so strange and bizarre that a fiction writer of macabre tales would have great difficulty trying to equal them.

A tale of ghosts and marvels, of the mighty ones who moved across the world stage and brought their hopes and fears to this twentieth century Seer. They showed him their palms, revealing the most intimate aspects of their personalities and looking to have him unravel the mysteries that their destinies had not yet revealed.

This gifted, nomadic man witnessed many wondrous events. Cheiro married late in life. At a chance meeting he once told a young girl, many years his junior, about her tragic first marriage, but that she would marry again — after a long time had passed — to a man she would meet again and again, in every far-flung corner of the world. And so she did. Her name was Mena, the woman destined to walk beside him in the latter part of that strange pilgrimage we call life. From the time she learned he was desperately ill and flew to his side to nurse him back to health, until his death twenty-five years later, they were rarely separated.

Seldom has there been a man whose rare gifts led him into such varied company and who felt so keenly the responsibility that those gifts entailed. Wherever I happened to go in my travels, whether as a musician or a mystic, the name of Cheiro inevitably comes up. Sometimes it was spoken with reverence, sometimes with scorn, usually by his "colleagues." Despite being a notorious womanizer and an Irishman who enjoyed his drink, he possessed a remarkable ability to predict the future of people by examining the lines on their hands. How many of those coming events were gleaned specifically from the study of hand reading, which indicates personality traits, and how many he saw in his mind's eye, has been the subject of much debate for many years.

His late wife, Countess Mena Hamon, once said the level of his sensitivity was so finely tuned that he could lock into the personal electro-magnetic force field of each individual and view the collected images of his past, present and future, much the same way we look at television and computer screens today. For certain the man had charisma, charm and good looks because women flocked to his drawing room to have him hold their hands and read their future. The more stories I heard about this extraordinary man from old-time celebrities he gave readings to, the more curious I became and I decided to learn as much as I could about this intriguing man. As *Fate* would have it, one of my clients, a former striptease artist, met and married a wealthy New York stockbroker who then taught her his trade, and made a small fortune based on one of my predictions. Out of gratitude, as Mary Kash put it, she brought me to New York where I arranged to meet and read the hands of legendary silent screen star Lillian Gish, then in her eighties. Gish knew Cheiro "very well," as she put it.

To step inside her apartment was to enter another era; a time and place far removed from today. A collection of soft and brightly colored vases from every period: a Victorian here, a Ming there; exquisite Royal Doulton figurines peeking out from behind fine filigree cabinet windows; upholstered Queen Anne chairs; a baby grand in one corner, the floor covered with Persian carpets, the walls and furniture adorned with family portraits and photos which created a who's who of old Hollywood: Lillian with her sister Dorothy, Clark Gable, Buster Keaton, Charlie Chaplin, Fatty Arbuckle, Elizabeth Taylor, Richard Burton, Eddy Cantor, Al Jolson and, of course, her creator D.W. Griffith, the premier movie producer of such silent epics as *Way Down East* and *Birth of a Nation*.

Looking elegant in an Oriental pant and smock outfit, Miss Gish served us tea and petit fours on fine bone china that seemed made of eggshells, it was so delicate, and said, "Cheiro was a real Count, you know. Very charming and very handsome. He used the prints of my hands in one of his first palmistry books." To this I immediately replied: "Yes, Ms. Gish, I know. That's why I'm here. I, too, want your handprints so that I can compare today's impressions with those that Cheiro took and note the changes." As she laid her palms in mine, I said: "I have nearly spanned the time barrier. When our hands touch, through you, the gap which separates Cheiro from me will at last be bridged." When I left, she gave me an original autographed copy of one of his earliest palmistry books.

I read her hands and made some predictions which later came true. She called me a few months later to say my predictions were so accurate that she wanted to see me again. I complied and at our next meeting she surprised me by saying: "Cheiro's widow, Countess Mena, gave me some of her personal papers for safekeeping and said Cheiro told her that one day I would meet someone who should have them. I now know you are that person."

As *Fate* would have it, when I returned to Toronto, I met with world renowned Hindu Palmist Mir Bashir who was on a world tour. He knew Cheiro very well and he recounted to me many of Cheiro's exploits and adventures. Over the years, I also have collected other letters, notes, essays and original photos and newspaper articles reporting on Cheiro's death and the ghostly events surrounding the passing of this remarkable man. His funeral was worthy of a Hollywood premiere. Almost eerily, as though again by a quirk of *Fate*, the responsibility of writing his life story fell to me. Here then, is the intriguing story of the life and times of the fascinating man known as Cheiro.

Anthony Carr, Toronto, January 2003

Chapter One

Out of the Mist

Tall, commanding and handsome, with deep-set, compelling eyes, Cheiro was kind, intuitive and — a rare combination — equally liked by men and relentlessly pursued by women. Bound by a self-imposed reticence, like a priest, he regarded the many secrets entrusted to him as the responsibilities of a confessional and he had the innate discretion of a courtier.

The seer-to-be was born at what was known as *The Priest's House*, near Bray, Ireland, on November 1, 1866, the elder of the two children of John William Le Warner, and his beautiful wife Margaret.

His forbears, of the Huguenot faith, were forced to flee to Ireland for their lives when the religious persecutions began in France. During this period, a ship slipped quietly out to sea with a handful of passengers who were fleeing their homeland rather than give up their faith. Chief among the party were Cheiro's grandparents: a French nobleman, his wife — the young countess — and an infant son, Cheiro's father. Except for a few pieces of jewelry, they became penniless foreigners in a strange land, without any hope of returning to their homeland.

Theirs was an ancient lineage reaching back to a pagan Scandinavian sea king named Hamon, who colluded with St. Helier of Jersey and later adopted the Christian faith in order to wed the daughter of a French King. The family was also associated with Rollo, a kinsman of William the Conqueror. As one of his nobles, Robert de Hamon accompanied William in his invasion of England, and was granted lands under the title Prince of Glamorganshire. He established the first monastery in England, Tewkesbury Abbey, and is still honored by a procession of distinguished clergy who make a pilgrimage once every hundred years round his tomb. Cheiro, the last descendant of his line, took part in this procession on March 25th, 1925, and gazed reverently at the tattered Hamon standard that still hangs in the Abbey.

The little vessel was cast up on the Irish shore and the priest of Bray harbor took them into his home. No doubt the priest found the Count, courtly and cosmopolitan, a stimulating companion and the refugees found a useful niche in their altered circumstances. But the fact remains they were dependent on the charity of a stranger — a priest of Rome, for their roof and bread — and, probably, for protection from pursuers of their creed. It must have rankled his ancestors. As a concession to *Fate* and maybe also to local prejudices and also to cover their tracks, they dropped their title and assumed a plainer style. Their financial situation eventually improved due to remuneration and legacies from wealthy families to whom the Count acted as tutor and slowly he acquired land and made investments which produced a modest income. During the ensuing years, the family built up a sizable estate, but nowhere close to its former glory when the Hamons had been wealthy aristocrats in France.

This child of John William and Margaret Le Warner Hamon was destined to become one of the greatest mystics in history — even surpassing, some say, the predictive abilities of Nostradamus and Cagliostro. He was encouraged in his studies of the occult by his mother, herself a gifted palmist, who examined his tiny hands at birth and prophesied: "My little son has the mystic cross prominently marked in both hands; for this reason I am giving to him all my books on hand analysis and numerology, for I believe that someday he will become a great prophet." An extremely beautiful woman of Greek and French extraction, she taught Cheiro all she knew about palmistry, and it was from her that he acquired this strange gift of second sight which would bring him fortune and fame. And, because precognitive ability is like a double-edged blade, it would also bring heartbreak and tragedy.

His father, a strict disciplinarian and now a well-to-do businessman, was horrified and bitterly opposed to Cheiro being connected to any superstitious nonsense. As the boy grew into a tall, thoughtful youth, it became apparent that he was not an ordinary child; he possessed a knowledge that belied his years and he gradually pieced together something of his curious family history, despite his father's reserve.

Louis was tutored by his father and the priest, and he showed early signs of remarkable mathematical ability. In an effort to wean his son from occult interests, his father sent Cheiro to a theological school to study for the Anglican priesthood, but to no avail, as the study of the hand continued to fascinate him.

Cheiro unexpectedly won the favor of one disciplinarian professor by reading his hand and unlocking long-kept, closely guarded secrets of happier days gone by. It happened one rainy day when he was kept in after class for some misdemeanor. The professor, curious at his absorption, crept up behind Cheiro and thrust his palms forward and said: "What do you make of these, young master Hamon?" He was so disturbed by the revelations that came tumbling from the schoolboy's lips that he treated his wayward pupil with indulgence, even translating for him ancient classical treatises on cheiromancy. Although the teacher was disliked by the student body because of his sternness, Louis told him of a love — a love so great that after her death the professor wanted to die and never loved anyone again. Great tears rolled down his cheeks as he patted the boy on the shoulder and slowly walked away.

After four years at the school, Cheiro had studied hard and rose to the top of his class. At seventeen he was chosen to make the valedictory speech. Two days before the commencement exercises, young Hamon awoke late one night, shaken and perspiring. The next morning he told the headmaster about a dream in which everything he had worked so hard for was suddenly taken from him!

"Nerves, my boy, all nerves," the teacher reassured him. "Pay no attention to it."

The next morning, in the room he shared with another student, Louis was preparing his speech when an envelope was delivered to him. It said his father had been ruined in a business speculation and that he was to return home immediately, as it was financially impossible to keep him in school. Numbed by shock, Louis read and reread the letter. Still holding the note that turned his world upside down, he sat and stared aimlessly out the window. As the full impact hit him, he was unable to hold back his tears.

His roommate, Richard Waterhouse, walked in to catch Cheiro trying to compose himself as the budding young mystic, born under the secretive zodiacal sign of Scorpio, did not want to appear foolish in front of his friend. This was a period in history when most of the world considered emotional displays by men — except anger — as something less than masculine.

"Hello Louis, I just wanted to — here now! What's this?" Richard asked, surprised by his friend's tears.

"Nothing. Really. But I do believe I'm catching the ague," he replied, in his unmistakably Irish accent.

Richard was typically English, and without pressing the issue read the letter sitting on the table, then placed a hand on Louis' shoulder:

"Dreadfully sorry, old man," then left Cheiro alone with his thoughts.

The next morning, when the graduating ceremonies got under way, another student made the valedictory speech. Louis Hamon was conspicuously absent.

The day wore on, twilight slipped into night and Louis, along with Richard and another friend, are roaming the Moorish countryside with several bottles of wine. It became very late and the three youths, feeling the effects of too much wine, explore an old cemetery. Everything is in darkness, except for a lighted candle carried by one of the boys. The young men were fascinated by an inscription on an ancient tombstone. They talked incessantly, wondering aloud what this or that person was like in life, whether they laughed, loved, cried.

"So then — this is the sum total of a man's life?" a frustrated Louis exploded. "After all the suffering? The sorrow? The hope? To end up beneath the sod, a moldering pile of bones? With no more than a chunk of granite over his head to remind the world that he once existed?"...

It must have been a strange spectacle to the night creatures, witnessing this unnatural gathering around a graveside in the dead of night. Yet at seventeen, Louis Le Warner Hamon was already expressing cynicism of a kind which usually doesn't become apparent until the battle of life has left its invisible scars.

The trio continued wandering among the old graves until they came to the site of a large mausoleum, a dome structure, built half underground and half above. One glance revealed that it hadn't been opened in many years; fungi, moss and other excrescences completely covered the building. The entrance was difficult to find because it was a stone slab that seemed to blend in with the building. Out of morbid curiosity, the three boys began pushing against it. All at once, the slab, held by a revolving hinge, gave way and swung round — sweeping one of the boys inside with it!

Louis Hamon, the young man the world would one day come to know as Cheiro, the seer, was trapped inside. A stream of moonlight poured through a crack in the ceiling, and the horrified Louis could see caskets which were not interred in vaults, but placed against the wall in a circular fashion. A stench of rotting bones, wood and clothing filled his nostrils. Frantically he threw his weight against the concrete door and tried to swing it back, while outside, his friends did likewise. Their efforts were in vain and they were forced to go for help. Six burly men were on their way to free the prematurely entombed youth when they saw him walking toward them.

"My God!" Richard exclaimed. "How did you get out?"

"I-I'm not sure. After you left, the door started moving — by itself! Or so I thought. But when I stepped out, an old man dressed in a purple cassock and wearing a large gold cross around his neck, greeted me.

"We walked along and he started talking — speaking in a voice that was strange, metallic, far-off sounding ...as though it wasn't really coming from him at all, but from somewhere else!

"He said I would go places and do things most men considered insane and that someday I would walk with Kings. Judging from the way he dressed and talked, I though him quite insane, but decided to humor him:

'What is your name?' I asked.

"I am George Berkeley."[1]

"When he said that, I could barely contain myself and turned away to laugh but when I turned back — he was gone! Yet, there were no buildings or trees for him to hide behind. And Richard — now that I think of it — when he spoke, his eyes didn't seem to be looking at me at all, but rather, through me."

"But Louis," Richard interjected, "you must— "

"And another thing he said — which seemed even more incredible — is that he knew I had a strange tailbone at the bottom of my spine, which is supposed to belong to persons of *Destiny*. Or so it is said; to those who may one day accomplish great things. Richard... absolutely no one but my family physician knows I am a caudate."[2]

"Louis," Richard interrupted, "you must know that Bishop George Berkeley was one of the greatest philosophers

---

[1] George Berkeley was an Anglican bishop remembered chiefly as a philosopher. He was born of English stock near Kilkenney, Ireland, on March 12, 1685 and died in 1753.

[2] A caudate's spinal column has two or three extra vertebrae causing the backbone to terminate below its normal point, creating the appearance of a tail.

and theologians who ever lived. However, my friend, he died nearly one hundred and fifty years ago!"

This was the first reported visitation of a specter to Louis Hamon, whose degree of sensitivity was so finely tuned that it clearly transcended earthly limitations.

Dawn's first light was filtering through when Louis returned to his quarters. Although completely exhausted after his nocturnal tirade of self-pity, while climbing the creaky old staircase leading to his room, the strange prophecies of the old gentleman in the cemetery began to fill Louis' mind.

Too upset and over-tired to sleep, he began packing. At seventeen, the charm and striking good looks which would make him a favorite at the courts of all the crowned heads of Europe and Hollywood, was already evident. One of his teachers, a clergyman, had made a homosexual advance that shocked the young seer, since he was not yet world-wise. He was raised to trust and respect people who were older and supposedly wiser than he was — especially the couriers of God's word. What was he to think now?

At such an impressionable age, the amorous advances by a respected professor of theology, coupled with the visitation in the cemetery, was enough to revolutionize the life, thoughts and beliefs of Louis Hamon. He rejected fundamental religion and began to conceptualize his own philosophy about reincarnation and *Divine Power*. Never again would he tread the well-worn path mapped out by church dogma. Louis finished packing, said good-bye to his friends, and made for home.

His parents, greatly concerned about the future of their son's education, suggested that he attend a local Roman Catholic theological seminary. This was favored by Louis' Roman Catholic mother, and temporarily solved the financial problem of how to resume his education. Although Louis had said nothing about the incident with the headmaster, he did tell his parents of the ghostly specter in the cemetery and about its predictions for their son — the son for whom the father had had such high hopes.

Louis told he father he wanted to make his own way in the world and dedicate his life to the study of the hand. Once again, the elder Hamon was livid! Following a heated argument, the young seer yielded in order to assuage his father's Irish temper. But Louis knew it would only be a matter of time until he left home.

Two more years passed, and it was the palmist who set the stage for his dismissal, once and for all. Each pupil was expected once a month to deliver a sample sermon in front of his professors and peers, by which he would be graded. Louis chose for his subject *The Hand of Judas Iscariot* and for 30 minutes he proceeded, in front of the horrified gathering, to describe Judas' personality as would have been indicated by the shape of his hands and the lines within.

The assemblage reacted as though struck by lightning. They listened in stunned silence while this student of theology, using the devil's implement — palmistry — expounded at length about the character of the man who betrayed Jesus Christ. After the explosion — and his expulsion — Louis once again returned home. He had undergone another mental metamorphosis. The apostate theologian now spurned the church; not the spiritual strength it represented, but the narrow mindedness and hypocritical attitude of the political machine that controlled it, namely the clergy.

This time, when the young mystic stood before his father, the elder Hamon now felt he no longer had the right to control his son's *Destiny* and gave his son his blessing and with a sigh of resignation said, "Go my son, go in peace. I have always known in my heart that you were meant for something else — perhaps something better. Wherever you go and whatever you do, Louis, remember that I love you."

Armed with nothing but this paternal blessing and a little money, Louis lost no time in departing. He shook the dust of Ireland from his feet, dust that held such an inexplicably strange sorrow and bitterness for him.

"For me, a mournfulness hung over the land, with its mists and melancholy blue mountains," he said years later. "These were times of terrible poverty and degradation in Ireland in my youth. The temper of the people was brooding and bitter. It seemed dreadful that the women, though so beautiful, should go about in shawls and bare, dirty feet. *Something* in me called for a refinement, an elegance *it* seemed to remember in place of this dreadful squalor, with pigs wandering in and out of the cabins."

"There goes one who will be a great occultist," his mother said, as he left, "a reincarnation, perhaps, of Cagliostro."

Without a backward glance or a nostalgic pause, he went forward, this time on a flood of inner assurance that an important role was to come to him. Louis set his face, a modern Dick Whittington, and made straight for London, the hub of the world, on the River Thames, to begin the first in a long series of bizarre adventures that would take him around the world. His true *Destiny*, prophesied by the spirit in the cemetery, was to spend his life travelling from one country to another.

It was a boy, not quite a man, who stood amid the hustle and bustle in the way station and waited for the train that would carry him the last leg of his journey to London. Louis looked down with apprehension, toward that mighty city in the distance.

As he was running to catch his train, he passed a newsstand and saw a paperback book about palmistry. It cost only a few coppers so he bought it to help while away the journey. Three other passengers occupied the coach with Louis: two men, one young, one middle-aged and a young woman.

The woman was blond and attractive with full, pink lips that gave her mouth a poutish look and she had the most beautifully almond shaped green eyes Louis had ever seen. Yet, what really caught his attention was her bosom. Indeed, he thought it was a wonder to behold. Their eyes met momentarily and a smile passed between them, but her smile was that of a confident young woman, secure in the knowledge that if she chooses, she could do what she wanted with this inexperienced young man.

The older man had sat beside Louis, but his face wasn't quite visible because of a muffler wrapped about his mouth and a top hat beneath which only a pair of cool, gray eyes could be seen.

However, everyone's attention was drawn to the younger man sitting beside the woman. He was a loud, boisterous American, so powerfully built that no one dared try to quiet him. He talked and joked and continually twirled his long, black handlebar mustache around his fingers.

"Well, m'bucko!" he bellowed in American slang, "What's that yer' readin' about — hands?!"

"Yes, yes I am," Louis replied.

"Well, then," the big man continued, "take a look at these, will ya?" — and he held out two hands that looked like shovels.

Quietly and coolly Louis examined the hands and said: "Obviously you are a man who makes his living with his fists. You are a violent, arrogant man, but you have a good heart. From the Line of *Fate* I can see much success. Yet, —

"I'm the best, m'boy, the very best!" he roared.

"Yes," Louis continued, "but I can see, from where the line begins to break up, when your career will come to an abrupt halt. It will be brought about by another Irishman."

"Never!" he shouted, shaking his fist, ranting and raving like a madman, until the train coasted into London's Euston station. The big American-Irishman got up to leave. He turned to Louis, his huge frame filling the compartment door, and good-naturedly said: "Listen, my fine fellow, unless you gain another twenty pounds and want to try me, there ain't another Irishman alive that's gonna tangle with the great, John Sullivan!"[3]

The legendary pugilist stepped from the train amid hundreds of cheering fans and well wishers, who had been waiting hours just to catch a glimpse of the champion.

Shortly after, the other three travelers left the compartment. Louis lingered a moment to help the lady with her luggage. As the couple shouldered their way through the streaming throngs, the young mystic was tapped on the shoulder. He turned to find himself face to face with the older gentleman from the train. The man removed his muffler, and in a soft spoken voice said: "Young man, may I speak with you a moment?"

"Certainly. What can I do for you?"

"I was rather interested in your interpretation of that pugilist's hands. Do you really believe that one's past and future can be determined by the lines in his hands — and if so, how?"

"Sir," Louis began, "I have always believed the hand to be the servant. When you think of an action to be performed, do you not follow through with your hands?"

---

[3] John L. Sulivan reigned as heavyweight champion of the world from 1881 to 1892. He was the last of the great bare-knuckle fighters and was defeated by "Gentleman" James Corbett, another Irishman, on March 15, 1892 at the Olympic Club, New Orleans.

"Yes, that is quite true," replied the man with the gray eyes.

"Therefore," the palmist concluded, "it should follow, according to my premise, that the unconscious mind will indicate future events, as well as record those which have already occurred."

"Hmmm...it does sound logical," he said, analyzing the theory. "Would it be too much of an imposition if I asked you to analyze my personality by your methods?"

"Certainly not."

They excused themselves from the lady, who had been watching and listening intently, and sat on one of the numerous benches around the station. Louis examined the hands, noting the long head-line, indicating a high intellect, and the strong thumbs, which told of a man with tremendous willpower — one who will see his plans through even unto death. He told the gentleman about major changes that had taken place in his past and then finished off with a character analysis.

"But tell me, young sir," he inquired with great reserve, although a modicum of anxiety could be detected, "you made mention of a brilliant past career attributed to the marking under my third finger, which you refer to as *The line of the Sun*; yet I notice that in both hands there is a cross at the top of each line. What does it mean?"

Louis did not answer right away. He thought for a moment, after which he decided to tell only part of his interpretation. With a facetious laugh, the uncomfortable youth replied: "Oh, that; well, that just means a rest from labor and toil...rather like an early retirement."

"But the cause — what will be the cause?" the man asked with growing impatience, allowing his facade to slip even further.

Looking him straight in the eye, Louis answered: "Without a doubt, a woman."

The gentleman put down his hands, and with a relaxed smile, said: "Young man, much of what you have told me about my past life has been remarkably accurate, but your prediction about a serious love affair is quite impossible. Here is my card. Now you will understand why such a liaison is out of the question. I am much too busy to allow a woman to interfere in my career. Good-bye, and thank you." The card read: Charles Stewart Parnell.[4]

Louis returned to the pretty lady who was still waiting for him, and as he reached down for her valise, she stopped him.

"You are a most fascinating young man. I have to leave now, but I do hope we meet again and can spend some time together." And by the way she looked at him, there was little doubt as to how that time would be spent. A strange hypnotic power belonged to this lad; and combined with charm and handsomeness, it left women helpless in his presence; a gift bestowed by the gods upon those precious few, yet highly sensitive souls who now and then sojourn on the earth plane.

"But what is your name?" Louis called after her. She walked away — smiled as she glanced over her shoulder. Through the din of the crowd he heard: "Ann Livingston."[5]

She waved, then disappeared into the crowd. The young adventurer went out into the streets of London. His worldly possessions consisted of an overnight bag, one suit of clothes that he had on his back, one shilling and a heart full of hope.

It was late morning and the city was teeming with life, people determined in their destinations and impatient to get there. Young Louis felt lonely and out of place and wandered around aimlessly. As the day wore on, he found himself in south London...the slums. After being besieged by panhandlers and prostitutes, the little money he had arrived with was gone, and hunger and fatigue were beginning to take their toll.

Night fell. Through the darkness the lone figure of a woman came towards him. It would be obvious to anyone what she was — to anyone that is, except a naïve youth.

---

[4] Charles Stewart Parnell, leader of the Irish Nationalist Party, born June 27,1846, died October 6,1891, it is said, of a "broken heart." After the scandalous O'Shea divorce trial, his career ruined, Parnell gave up the ghost.
[5] Ann Livingston, Sullivan's mistress, accompanied him to England. At the time, the law did not allow women to attend boxing matches. So whenever the champ defended his title, she would don men's clothing, wait until the fight was well under way and show up.

"'ello, luv. Yer looking a bit lonely, ... ere now, you are a 'andsome one, ain't cha?"

"Oh, uh...well, thank you," he stammered. Sidling up to him, she asked the age-old question in an unmistakable cockney accent: "D'ya fancy a bit a'company tonight, luv?"

"I, uh, that's very kind of you," Louis struggled; not yet fully comprehending, but suddenly feeling very much like a little boy. "But I really cannot afford to...to take you to...dinner."

"Dinner is it! You really are new around here, ain't 'cha, Luvey?" She laughed hysterically, then abruptly stopped. The hard-core lady of the night looked at the hapless brown eyes, and was moved: " 'ave you eaten today, luv?"

"No," he lamely replied.

Shaking her head, she took him by the arm and led him along" C 'mon,' andsome, I'll take care of ye," and he followed her through the dark, dank alleyways.

Louis spent the night with her, and the next morning, as he meandered along the docks of Tilbury, he carried himself with the air of a cocky young man, very sure of himself....

The docks were brimming with activity when Louis arrived. He looked out of place as he sat on a tall pile of rope and watched in awe at the great ships coming and going — loading and unloading their precious cargo. But it was the ships from far off lands that intrigued him most. Louis tried to guess where they came from by the exotic names painted on their hulls. He had long nurtured a secret desire to visit India, where inexplicable events occur everyday and miracles are considered commonplace.

There, he could pursue his palmistic studies without condemnation. Queen Victoria was still on the British throne and palmistry was not considered a noble profession for a young man to follow.

Louis lingered around the docks until he found a ship that was bound for India. The ship's company was too busy loading cargo to notice the tall youth walking up the gangplank, as was the captain who was scowling and intently checking figures. He was a fierce looking man with a ruddy complexion, and a nose even redder from too much liquor.

Louis tentatively approached the Captain while he was barking orders and swearing soundly — to himself and his men — obviously frustrated by the paperwork. Louis picked this importune moment to speak:

"Excuse me, sir, but I would like to go to sea."

The captain looked up abruptly — his eyes blazing with anger at having been interrupted. He exploded: "What! Go to hell! — And get off my goddamn ship!"

As soon as the young would-be adventurer recovered from the blistering attack, he attempted to do just that. But when he turned to leave he was shocked to find the gangplank raised and realized to his horror that the ship had quietly slipped away from the pier!

The flabbergasted youth decided to disappear until everyone had settled down. He hid in a lifeboat until dark, and it was only hunger that made him venture forth. Louis mustered together all his courage and headed for the captain's cabin. The astonished captain looked up from his messy desk which he was still hunched over — still cursing the paperwork — and bellowed:

"What the blue blazes are you doin' here?!" Just as Louis thought he was about to be thrown overboard, the master of the ship suddenly glanced down at the mess in front of him, back up at Louis, looked him straight in the eye, and asked: "You any good with figures?" Louis was given a job as the ship's bookkeeper, and because of his likable disposition and ability to read hands, he quickly won the friendship of the rough seamen.

When the day's work was done, many a night they would lie on the forward deck and tell him of their homes, wives, and sweethearts. He read their hands but he could not see their futures...not for even one man!

It was a long, tedious voyage and the last port-of-call was Bombay, often referred to as the "Gateway to India." He bade farewell to his friends and the next morning the ship set sail for England.

Louis was destined to spend several years in India, years so different from the Western habits of life that he was used to and he was completely cut off from his familiar world.

It wasn't until three years later that he learned, by chance, that the ship he had sailed on to Bombay had foundered and sunk on its homeward passage. All hands were lost. Not until Louis showed up in London years later did his family discover that he didn't perish as well and stop mourning him as dead.

Chapter Two

A Mystic's Education

Anticipation was tinged with fear when Louis found himself in a strange land, entirely dependent on his own resources. He had not yet displaced the sorrow he felt at parting from his rough, but good-hearted sailor friends. Surrounded by the noise, jostle, color and exotic new smells of an Indian morning in Bombay, he made his way to a stone seat at the end of a pier and sat down to collect his thoughts.

He had wanted to get away from familiar scenes and his cramped surroundings to travel and see the world's wonders but perhaps, like many a cloistered youth, scarcely believed he was actually there. Yet here he was. *Destiny* had brought him here to this place! But what to do next? He was caught up in a mêlée of strange tongues, colors, and creeds. He was entirely alone in that mass of humanity. Feelings of helplessness began sweeping over him.

However, one person was aware of his presence. An old man, clad in some kind of priestly garb, advanced towards him. A surprisingly pleasant voice uttered in English, "Good morning."

To the lonely boy, this was like money from home. The old man began the conversation with commonplace remarks — the splendid view of the bay, the town, the interest of the throng. Then, in response to Louis' statement that he had arrived only that morning, he turned to the lad with the direct question:

"Why did you come to India?"

Louis replied that it had always been his earnest desire, and added — pointing to the Line of *Fate* in his right hand — "Besides, I suppose I am just following my *Destiny*."

With a strange look, the old man held out his hands towards Louis, saying, "You have been reading hands for years? Read mine. I very much would like to see your European palmistry."

Louis was nervous and disinclined to show his little knowledge before such a mystic, such an adept, but he seemed so kind and sympathetic that Cheiro resolved to do his best and went about the task with all the earnestness he possessed. He did not speak till Cheiro had completely finished. Then he quietly said: "your hand reading is good. Come away with me from this noise and clamor to solitude, peace and study, amid the mysteries of India and of *Nature.*"

For a moment Cheiro hesitated. He had no friends in India, no career, no responsibilities in life. What would it matter if he never came back? No one would miss him. He would only be one of the many that rise and fall and are lost to sight in the great ocean of humanity. The next second he said: "I am ready. I will go with you."

"Good," answered the mysterious stranger. "I will now show you your home."

So saying, he pointed to a mountain that rose higher than all the rest and seemed a long way off in the distance.

"That is Parbul," he said. "On its flat top, thousands of years ago, Vishnu spoke to mortals. We will start now. Near there will be your home."

Four days later Cheiro found himself far up on the heights of Parbul and learned that an underground Hindu temple was to be his new home. For how long he did not know.

But he did know that India has long been the home of mystery and learning. It is to this country that we trace the world's oldest civilization, the oldest scriptures, and the commencement of all written language. There is no other country in the world that has produced such spiritual sacrifices; no race that has equaled these people in their study of *Nature* in all its intricacies and mysteries. Knowledge is power; so it follows that with the knowledge they have obtained they also have the power to command *Nature* by subtle means not dreamt of by ordinary people. Hypnotism, as practiced by Brahmins, is unexplained by any known laws that the greatest scientists have yet discovered. It has been demonstrated that even over animals they exercise power in a way that baffles the most astute researchers.

The temple that Cheiro lived in was one of the oldest of the cave temples that are the relics of ancient India. It was tenanted by a small class of Brahmins who were celebrated for the mysteries they practice. They kept aloof from all other sects and very seldom came in touch with ordinary people. The temple was presided over by a council of seven, of which Cheiro's friend had the highest position due to his age and learning. Without his aid, it would have been impossible for

Cheiro to gain their confidence and friendship. He continued his occult studies under the Brahmin Priests because he had demonstrated some palmistic and clairvoyant abilities.

One night the seven Brahmins were preparing for a mystic ceremony that was to take place at midnight. By then, Cheiro had seen a great number of these seances and recognized that this would be something unusual. He resolved not to ask permission to see it, but to try to do so by concealing himself in some corner of the cave temple they arrived at after walking for hours through a dense forest.

Midnight came. Cheiro crept from his hiding place to find everything ready, and the ceremony commenced. In the centre of the temple and before a great idol of Shiva (the Destroyer) he saw the seven seated in a large circle, about three feet between each. In the centre, lying on the ground naked, with his head toward the north, was a young boy about twelve years old, conscious but motionless. The temple, which was of considerable size and hewn out of ancient solid rock, was entirely in darkness except for the faint light given by four braziers, smoldering under herbs and incense, outside the circle. The stillness of death seemed to fill the place.

The Daghope (altar) stood out in bold relief from the surrounding gloom. This was due to a peculiar aperture cut through the solid rock to the outer world. It was shaped like a horseshoe and was placed so that the light from the skies fell day and night on this underground altar. At noon, the beams of sunlight were intensely brilliant but even on the darkest of nights some light used to penetrate. At this particular moment, the light of a full moon turned the night into day and streamed through the aperture, increasing the brilliancy of that one spot.

The Brahmins had changed their positions. Instead of sitting they were lying, face downward, eyes fixed on the body of the boy, their arms outstretched fully and pointing along the ground like needles toward their victim. It was a terrible sight. Their eyes were flashing with earnestness, while the deadly stillness of the place was horrible in its intensity. Up to this moment they had not spoken. Slowly and steadily the boy seemed to sink into unconsciousness. Suddenly his body began to writhe in agony and his eyes stared out from their sockets! There was a gurgle, a sob, and a sigh. Then the writhing ceased as abruptly as it began. His head fell back motionless. The spirit had been freed from his body and sent to the outer world to obey the wishes and will of the Brahmins.

At the moment the spirit of the boy tore itself free of his body, the Brahmins started a low, monotonous chant. It seemed to rise from the earth on which they lay, sobbed and moaned among the pillars and idols, then died away in the shadows, like the crying of a child. All was silent again. Then darkness. The moonlight had passed away and even the braziers seemed to die away.

In the distance there was a thunderous roar in some far off part of the jungle. It was the sound of the most feared animal in India, an animal that, at the very mention of its name, strikes terror into the hearts of people, the man-eating Bengal Tiger! The group redoubled its intensity. Again they began their strange chant which wailed and sobbed, then died away. Again the roar of the tiger, but this time — closer! This was repeated over and over. Each time, it was answered by the tiger — but with a different significance ... the roar of defiance gave way to a cry, a whine of fear, a moan of submission. And closer and closer came the sound of the tiger. From the darkness at the mouth of the cave there appeared a pair of fiery red eyes, followed by the head of the mighty Bengal Tiger! All eyes were transfixed. It was ferocious and horrible-looking against the black night sky!

The great brute entered the cave, step by step. His great eyes gleamed in the darkness as he slowly approached the circle. Suddenly the animal stopped at the very spot where Cheiro sat petrified! Those great orbs of fury turned to where he lay crouched in terror! The tiger's whole body bristled with rage and its teeth glistened as it got ready to spring, when the low, monotonous chant started again. The animal's eyes darted over toward the circle, its head dropped, and the tiger advanced, drawn on by some irresistible force.

By now it was so close to the circle that one of its paws was between the legs of one of the holy men. Slower and slower the tiger moved toward the prostrate body of the boy, as though it had no will of its own. The chant grew louder and louder — then, passing between their motionless forms, the tiger lay down across the body of the boy who appeared to be dead. The Brahmins lay motionless with their arms pointed toward the two corpse-like entities in the middle of the circle, but their eyes concentrated upon the body of the tiger.

As the chanting reached fever pitch — their voices all joining together in one tremendous sound — the Brahmins sprang to their feet and lashed themselves into a state of frenzy! At that moment the smoldering braziers leapt into heat and life and in the lurid light of their flames the Brahmins looked like demons dancing to the fires of hell!

The black rocks of the temple — carved with figures of animals and men seemed alive and horrible, dancing on the walls as the flames rose and fell within the braziers. The wild figures of the Brahmins, the frenzy of their movements, the chant, weird and terrible, sobbed and screamed, echoed and re-echoed, clashed and crashed through the idols that looked like humans, mocking and reveling in such a scene. It was beyond reason! And within all of this, the central point of the whole thing, sat Death! Grim. Silent. Wonderful. And beneath, as on his throne, lay the bodies of the boy and the tiger.

Then the leader, Cheiro's friend, sprang forward, rolled the body of the tiger over and plunged a knife into it below the neck — ripping it in two with one stroke! Quick as a flash, the intestines were torn out, still quivering with life, and thrown into the flames. The body of the boy was forced into the body of the tiger and the skin was drawn together. Then louder, wilder and fiercer than before, the chant rose higher and higher! The braziers lapped up the pools of blood with their flames. Then the smell of the burning flesh overcame Cheiro and he sank senseless to the ground.

When he recovered, Cheiro found they had looked after him carefully. They knew of his presence throughout their ceremony; but once it started they dared not break it. For the entire length of his stay afterwards, he was permitted to see whatever he chose.

Why was all this done? To endow the boy, a follower of their sect, with power over animals. The next day, when he was released from the body of the tiger, the boy seemed possessed of a power that was not human. From that moment on, fire could not hurt him, animals could not injure him and the deadliest snake in his hands became harmless; he passed through the jungle unharmed, and gave exhibitions of his powers to show the wonders that had been worked by his masters. Cheiro felt this was simply a case of hypnotism. His belief was so great, that he had absolutely no fear.

In this austere, ascetic regime, now and then violently punctuated by intense, dramatic episodes like this one, years passed. Cheiro was at last judged fit to pass through a rigorous initiation. But there was always the danger it might prove too much for him to endure, so he was first granted a vision of home and all he had left behind. Dimly, then more clearly, a wonderful picture emerged, the old familiar scene.... He saw his family house, his parents, his sister, the family pet — and was surprised to notice an aunt, who seemed to be living there, although that had not been the case when he left home. His parents were alive and well; though they seemed rather worn and sad, and his sister appeared even more delicate than before. It was with a twinge of regret that he now understood that since his departure, life had gone on for them as before. They probably missed him — but time marched on.

Cheiro successfully completed his initiation ordeal and his new life continued without further interruption, until one day an injured officer was carried in to rest and was forced by his injuries to remain for some time. He was an Irish officer serving with a regiment that was quartered nearby. Imagine the soldier's surprise to discover that among these strangely arrayed mystics, was a white man — and an Irishman at that — from his same corner of the Emerald Isle! Learning Cheiro's identity, he lost no time in telling him that all his family had given him up for dead when they heard that the ship on which he had sailed to India sank with all hands lost, on its homeward journey.

When Cheiro finally left his Indian preceptors, who said he had come to the end of his studies, he made a solemn promise that should he engage in cheiromancy as a profession, he would follow it with faith and devotion for 21 years and by his conduct, raise it in public esteem to the place of honor it had once occupied in the distant past. Little did he think that he would actually follow such an occupation but he made the vow and ended up faithfully keeping it. Indeed, circumstances thrust him back into cheiromancy time and time again over the years because the ability and skill that he displayed in deciphering the unknown for strangers, deserted him when dealing with his own future, no matter how gilt-edged and safe the projects appeared to be. Well might Oscar Wilde later say: "For Cheiro, the mystery of the world is the visible, not the invisible."

He bade a final farewell to India and went home to claim an inheritance from his aunt, who died, and left a substantial legacy of £20,000 to her nephew.

Chapter Three

Egypt

Louis came back to Europe as one raised from the dead, and as such was well-received by his stern father, devoted mother and delicate little sister. They were struck dumb. They had mourned his loss and found the aloof young mystic even more difficult to understand than before his return from the dead!

It wasn't long before the stifling atmosphere got to him again. He hated being on bad terms with the people he cared about. Yet he felt he had to once more follow his *Destiny*. He was still a very young man, fresh from his seclusion and his mystical experience in India. Now, for the first time in his life, he had the financial security to do what he wanted.

When he first went abroad, it was almost directly from one priestly environment to another, although the outward trappings were different. Now, as then, he wanted to wander, to explore the world and its mysteries untrammeled by sordid poverty. The mystical side of his *Nature* was still uppermost, but the fleshpots of the world were beginning to beckon, especially since he was at that age. He left Ireland for England, staying mainly in London, but also traveled throughout the country visiting various institutions, asylums and jails to collect a library of hand impressions.

Although he regarded the subject as a hobby, the study of the hand was his main preoccupation. To unearth the past and foresee the future but more than that, to observe through the *Web of Destiny* and see patterns emerge and to trace cause and effect, as well as the function of free will, these were the things that fascinated him. He established himself in the heart of London and tentatively tasted its pleasures while trying to retain something of the student's outlook. His long course of Spartan simplicity in the East caused him, after a little time, to feel a certain distaste for the trivialities of the West, enhanced no doubt, by the damp and gloom of English winter skies.

"For years my home had been an old temple cave," wrote Cheiro, "carved out of solid rock by a now forgotten race, that one finds in so many parts of that strange land of mystery. My only food was a diet of fruit and rice and my only companions a few men who had given up the world, the flesh and, perhaps, the devil."

He struck up a friendship with an old German Egyptologist, Prof. Von Heller, who was attached to the British Museum. The professor admired and deciphered the hieroglyphics on an ancient Persian ring worn by Louis that had been given to him in the East.

The professor was about to start for El Karnak to press forward the discovery of another Tomb of the Pharaohs. Facilities to do so were his reward for having diagnosed its existence and possible whereabouts from certain relics and jewels of a known period which had unexpectedly appeared on the market — stolen, it was assumed, by Arab grave robbers. Cheiro offered to join the party and, to his joy, was accepted as the old man's assistant.

Here again his mystical education took another turn. Under Egyptian skies he learned of the past greatness of her rulers and their efforts to preserve their people and their memory, only to be foiled by *Time*, as the centuries slowly passed and the desert sands softly piled up a mountain of oblivion.

Again, like steel to a magnet, fantastic experiences were attracted to him. There was the horrifying experience of being buried alive in the Pharaoh's newly discovered tomb, led there by an unhappy victim of the fickle finger of *Fate*, the man with a living snake growing out of his side! There was the strange gift of the mummy's hand, which was to accompany him for years, fulfilling its *Destiny* and protecting his. And there was the prophecy of the loss of his inheritance, which soon proved to be, alas, all too true.

He and the professor were swung wildly through a gamut of emotions — wonder, achievement, fear, horror, despair and a veritable resurrection, only for Louis to be plunged immediately afterward into the anticlimax of poverty once more. The professor, on the other hand, was to some extent insulated from these effects by his overwhelming absorption in Egyptian lore, but the young seer had no such protection.

Arriving at El Karnak, they established headquarters and bargained with local inhabitants for accommodation and guides. Once they found guides and put a party together, they set out across the Nile, bound for the Valley of Death and the Tombs of the Kings. In the early dawn, surrounded by silent relics of past kingly splendor, disturbed by an occasional bat which flew out blindly into the light of day, Louis contemplated the transitoriness of human life and the powerlessness of the individual, no matter how great he be, in his short span of years on this immense human chain.

The newcomers believed themselves alone, but soon discovered that their vigil was shared by a motionless young European, an Englishman, who disappeared into one of the tombs, on their approach. Cheiro relates this strange tale: "We saw him fleetingly many times, but he always avoided us, and we later learned from our guide that he was a recluse, a student — and brave — having rescued a little native girl from being crushed by the paddle wheel of a Nile steamer. The guide told us, however, that the young man was extremely afraid of snakes.

On one occasion, while wandering alone through the deserted Halls of Columns, they heard the most terrible moans of agony and discovered that they came from the young Englishman. He suddenly fell senseless across one of the stone figures in the hall! The others hurried forward to do what they could. All their efforts seemed in vain. However, they suddenly noticed some movement inside the man's open silk shirt. Thinking his breathing had become erratic; Cheiro opened his shirt...and was horrified! He saw that it was caused by a snake-like growth, living like a parasite on its human host! The shock was too much. The old Professor led Cheiro away in a daze. The young man, meanwhile, recovered and made off without a word. When at last Cheiro was well enough to recount what he had seen, the Professor wouldn't believe it!

Gradually, their research went on, in spite of treachery by their guides who were anxious to grab Egypt's secrets for their own profit. And although the professor felt himself on the eve of great discoveries, the final clue eluded him. He was in despair when their mysterious young acquaintance, who had already furnished them with one important link and then retreated, as aloofly as before, suddenly came forward and volunteered himself to guide them to the tomb they sought.

At this stage he urged the utmost secrecy, as the tomb's location was known only to him and a few Arabs, and they regarded it as a treasure trove. "I cannot take the glory of its discovery myself," he said. "I have been waiting for someone who would realize its historic and scientific value before revealing it."

At night, cautiously avoiding observation and carrying no lighted lanterns, they made their way through the moonlight and the shadows to the appointed meeting place. A presentiment of evil passed over them even though at first all seemed well.

They passed through the now familiar labyrinth. In a small carved chamber that appeared to lead nowhere, their new friend showed them where to place their feet. On a certain faintly worn mark in the rock, by exerting light pressure on the wall the entire side swung back, revealing a similar rock-hewn chamber beyond. With an equally light touch after crossing the threshold, the wall swung back into position, and they were left, unobserved, or so they thought, to go on through the chamber, along a narrow passage and down a kind of tunnel, on whose upper edge was balanced precariously, a huge block, like a logan stone.

All at once Cheiro realized its dire purpose — that it could easily be dislodged! He felt a moment's disquiet at the thought that the slightest touch from a malevolent pursuer would sent it hurtling down to the small aperture below, sealing the tomb they were about to enter. They passed through the dark hole and paused under a small archway, awestruck by the vast grandeur of the hollow, seven-sided pyramid tomb, which they found themselves in where the seven mummies were partly despoiled of their treasures. Then a fiendish laugh reached them, awaking strange echoes in the marble hall, and a reverberating crash told them -- too late -- that their unseen followers had moved the stone into position. They were sealed in the tomb.

They only just had time to note the scattered jewels looted from the partly unwrapped mummies. The professor had thrilled to the prospect that here, in the one unrifled sarcophagus, might be the long sought body of Cheops, missing from the Great Pyramid. Then they saw a man's skeleton spread-eagled on the floor, arrested by an unknown hand in the very act of fleeing with the jewels his fingers were clutching.

It seemed likely that this place would become their grave as well, for nobody knew they were there! They explored every inch of their prison but could find no exit. The feeble light from their lanterns could not penetrate very far into the depths of the central wall, which was a feature of the tomb, as in the Pyramids at Cairo. The lanterns dimmed and they began to suffer from the cold temperature of the tomb.

Shivering in the darkness, their companion full of remorse at having brought them to this plight, they heard him repressing the moans that heralded another of his strange attacks. He crept into a far corner to suffer alone. When the spasm passed, they drew him back into their company, in the shelter of the central coffer, whose discovery might have meant so much. Ever respectful of his reserve, they had not alluded to his suffering. But to their surprise, he began to tell his strange story, and in their pity for him they forgot for a moment the horror of their own *Fate*:

"My father," the poor man began, "was a colonel in the Indian Army, stationed in the north near the Afghanistan frontier. He had married rather late in life, the daughter of a fellow officer; a lady well equipped to handle the social side of his life. But she was extremely proud and intolerant, especially toward native customs and the holy men who abounded in the region. As a result, she earned much ill will locally. When circumstances pointed to a disastrous surprise raid that was caused by the most celebrated of the district's Yogis, she insisted on his execution, and on being present when it was carried out!

"Urged to confess, the Yogi asserted his innocence and willingness to die, at the same time warning her that neither she nor the child she carried would be able to escape, in turn, their own *Fate*. Her crime in demanding his punishment would bring about her own.

"As the guns fired, she screamed and fainted dead away in her husband's arms. Neither of them would reveal what had so startled her at that moment, but something had leapt from the ground and struck her!

"The child was prematurely born, and as soon as the new mother was well enough to travel, she surprised everyone who knew how ambitious she was, by demanding that her husband retire from the Army and settle in England. The boy grew up in the heart of Devon. The evening before I went to college, my father told me about the incidents that preceded my birth. My father then returned to India, but could not prevail upon my mother to join him.

"Scholastic honors came easily, and wherever I went, people predicted a brilliant future for me. I was looking forward to my father's long leave so we could discuss what career I should follow. I was also anxious to get his consent for betrothal to my childhood playmate, Lucy, the vicar's daughter, because my mother was bitterly opposed to the match"

As luck would have it, a fatal accident claimed the father before he arrived home and the boy discovered that the administration of the estate had been left to his mother, his only immediate direct prospect of property being a recently acquired tea plantation. Finding her still adamantly against his marriage plans, he decided to go to India to try and stop her from selling the plantation before he became of age. She begged him not to go to India — "Anywhere but there!" But still, she remained deaf to his entreaties to give her consent to his engagement.

"And so to India I came, but all sorts of minor hindrances plagued the completion of this business. On the morning of my twenty-first birthday I awoke from an eerie dream, with a curious throbbing pain in my side. I thought my father had appeared to whisper a message: 'The seed that is sown must be reaped — it matters little by whom. Be patient, there is no law but that of God. *Nature* and *Destiny* are servants thereto.'

"My Lucy's letters — at first more cheerful as my mother had become friendly and seemed to have withdrawn her opposition — began to change and lessen in their expressions of affection and hope. I then learned from her father that she was ill. This damnable business of mine dragged on and on, and I continued to suffer from this mysterious, agonizing pain in my side, but always deferred treatment, hoping it would pass."

He found himself within easy reach of his birthplace, and so with a few spare days before he could sail for home, his affairs at last concluded, he went there, made himself known, and received a cordial welcome from the colonel and his officers at the barracks. The old drama was recalled and the cave of the old Yogi, who had been shot, was pointed out to him. He suggested visiting it and some of the younger officers agreed to accompany him. All admired the little terrace with its garden of herbs and magnificent view "enough to make a mystic of any man who lived there."

On a slab in the simply appointed interior was this inscription in English: "No man shall escape his *Fate* — did not even a God die that the scriptures might be fulfilled?" They didn't like the atmosphere of the cave and hurried out to join the colonel who was waiting for them below. But young Chanley had forgotten his whip. Returning for it, he was shocked when he saw the apparition of the Yogi, pointing to the slab, whose words re-echoed through the young man's mind. He bolted from the cave, slipped on the rocks and fell down the precipitous slope, dislodging boulders and bushes in the process.

When he awoke he found himself in the colonel's quarters, after days of unconsciousness, suffering from cuts, bruises and a broken leg. He was obliged to cancel his passage and again heard of the grave illness of his Lucy, though the nature of her malady was not disclosed.

Meantime, the strange recurrent pain in his side had aroused the attention of the doctors. Then, after a particularly savage bout of agony, the flesh suddenly opened and a malevolent growth began to appear! They refused to continue with the case and had him conveyed to the nearest military hospital. Diagnosed as a rare tumorous growth, it was considered too near the vital organs to operate. It continued to develop and Chanley, as soon as his broken leg permitted, set sail for England, hoping for better medical advice in Europe, all the while wracked with anxiety about Lucy's health.

Rummaging through some of his father's old things during the voyage, he came across a diary of the months preceding his birth. There he read that "as the Yogi fell, a black snake sprang from the ground and struck his mother's side, afterwards disappearing as quickly as it came."

"It was then that a terrible sense of foreboding overcame me, and I felt an unexpected sickening movement at my side. I went below, and for the first time dared look at this monstrous thing that ceaselessly plucked at me...."

His worst suspicions were confirmed. It had quickened and was now a living, growing snake he carried with him! The surgeons in London gave him no hope. They could not kill the monstrosity without killing him. All they could suggest was to wait until it had developed sufficiently and then extract the poison fangs. Like an automaton he journeyed down to Devon, only to find Lucy on her deathbed, driven to despair by his mother who had reported his unfaithfulness in a final effort to separate them. He barely had time to convince her of his love before she died. At least she had been spared his dreadful news.

Bitter and resentful, he confronted his mother who admitted her actions had been prompted by jealousy and ambition. In despair, he laid bare that which had killed ambition and even hope itself in him. "I saw her look of revulsion, but it was only a reflection of my own self-loathing, and rushed away to endure my shame, in solitude."

Rudderless, his wanderings eventually led him to Egypt, finding in its impersonal sadness some measure of comfort and solace; a sweet oblivion in a land that eventually swallowed up even those mighty pharaohs who had striven so passionately to be personally remembered. It was his notion to be entombed as they were, since he felt his time had come, there, in the interminable darkness, his rest undisturbed by prying eyes, for all eternity. He rejected earlier thoughts of suicide in fear that his remains would be discovered, put on public display, and ridiculed; or, worse still, that his parasite would somehow survive! But now, he had unwittingly involved others in his *Fate*....

His story aroused deep pity in his listeners. A life, which seemed so full of promise, had been filled with disappointment, bitterness and waste. They lay there in silent sympathy, trying to summon up enough resignation to meet their end, while they lit a pile of linen strips that had once swathed a royal mummy. By its brief blaze they noticed the phosphorescent glow of a ring on a mummy's hand. The hieroglyphics it bore proved to be a plan of the passages radiating from this secret tomb and Chanley saw notches indicated in the wall of the well. Seizing the only possibility of escape, Chanley left his friends in an effort to find them a way back to life!

The professor had often told Louis that a similar well in the great Pyramid of Cheops led nowhere, so the chance of success was slim. As minute followed minute they waited and listened, feeding the dwindling fire with the last shreds of fuel. Still, their companion did not return. At last they heard a faint gasp; he had climbed over the edge of the well and collapsed. He was ragged and exhausted and had the mark of death on him. But, he managed to stammer instructions on which passages would take them to the Nile and to safety.

"But you must come with us, my boy," urged the old man, almost crying.

A slight movement of his hand waving them away was all Chanley could manage. He tried to smile, and feebly pointed to his side. The snake was burying its fangs in his flesh!

"Leave me here," he gasped as he clasped their hands. "The seed that was sown is gathered...Goodbye...."

This was actually the second time Louis and the professor had emerged from a living tomb. On the first occasion they were rescued by an Egyptian guide Louis had befriended, and succeeded in sending an appeal by thought transference to the guide to come and rescue them. During their two years of research this guide remained completely loyal to them. On the eve of their departure he begged Louis to accompany him for the last time to one of the ruined temples.

He said he had something to give him — "But I must give it to you alone." Without giving it a second thought, Louis went with him. The guide entered an excavation under the broken Sphinx. In the bundle the Egyptian passed over to Louis when he came out was the mummified hand of a woman bearing a carved gold ring on its finger. The hand was in perfect condition. The old guide explained that its existence had been revealed to him by his father, a descendant of a long line of Egyptian priests. He said it was that of the seventh daughter of King Akhnaton who had been succeeded by Tut-Ankh-Amen. His daughter had followed the strange new religion initiated by her father and was killed in battle against Thebes. The priests severed the hand that held the sword, embalmed it, and placed it in their temple as a warning.

A curse rested on the hand. It was doomed to wander through this world and be exhibited to all nations, until the lost tomb of her brother was discovered. The Egyptian said that it was Louis' *Fate* to fulfill part of this curse as the bearer of the hand on its worldwide pilgrimage. He foretold that Louis would always be a wanderer without a permanent home; that during his absence in Egypt his money would be taken from him; and that he would become a teacher of occult studies which would allow him to meet kings and world rulers.

He made Louis swear to guard the hand with his life and always carry it with him. In return, it would unfailingly protect him from danger. Awed by the man's solemnity and abrupt change to an authoritative manner, after months of subservience, Louis gave his promise.

Early next morning the Egyptian bade them adieu as they started on their journey, adding only this to Louis: "I know you will keep your promise."

At Cairo, the half-expected blow fell: Louis heard that the man he had left in charge of his affairs had misappropriated all his funds; and then committed suicide. At his wits' end, he was forced to turn to his knowledge of the hand in order to make a living. His first success was with the wife of the proprietor of the hotel where he was staying. Her husband chanced to overhear some of the palmist's revelations concerning her past, confronted her, and when she tearfully admitted they were true, forgave her and permitted her, with the young seer as her escort, to seek throughout the city for her child by a former lover, a child for whom she was still mourning.

This sensational success was publicized and Cheiro was soon overwhelmed by would-be clients. He earned enough to pay his way back to England, to look into his affairs. But of affairs, there were none! The first part of the Egyptian's prophecy had proved all too true — and nothing about the future was certain, except its uncertainty. He faced it with slim resources — save for youth, a reasonable supply of health, a lot of hope, which only the young can possess and, of course, the mummy's hand.

Chapter Four

The Gay Nineties

Back in London once more, almost penniless, Louis' thoughts turned somewhat bitterly to his two previous visits there. In 1882, as a 16 year old, he had listened to the hostile roar of the big city going about its business, oblivious of the hopes and fears of the lonely young man in its midst. Yet, one of those wide flung enterprises had enabled him to have the first pages of his incredible life story written in India.

Then unexpectedly, *Dame Fortune* smiled and when he was twenty, on his second visit, Louis was better equipped with experience, age and money to heed London's siren call. But the call of the East was still strong. And so here he was, a young man of the Western world, 23 years of age with some mystic and archaeological experiences in India and Egypt behind him, a knowledge of and aptitude for the study of the hand, but with no other training and still undecided as to how to earn a living.

First he turned to journalism, writing articles and verse of a devotional nature which met with considerable success. He lived simply in the top room of a seven-story building overlooking the embankment and began feeling proud of his independence. But soon his literary vein petered out. Fleet Street editors, notably the Rev. Richardson of *Great Thoughts* found his style so changed and so much more worldly that he could hardly believe the writer was the same person. Realizing it was, he was urged to abandon the bad influences that were luring him and his writing along the forbidden road but in the meantime, declined his contributions.

Cheiro had a nature that flourished and bloomed on encouragement. His work had been criticized unfairly, he thought; yet so far as he was aware, his outlook was unchanged. His confidence was sapped, and he felt drained and without resources. Nor did he know which way to turn or what to do next. Trudging back past Somerset House to his embankment flat and pondering his predicament, he noticed that a young man, in passing, stared fixedly at him.

So unproductive were his reflections on his own problems that he shelved them and allowed this trivial incident to set him off on another line of thought and then he was touched on the shoulder and turned to confront this same man, who had followed him!

"You don't remember me?"

"I can't say that I do."

"Well, I have reason to remember you. You read my hands in Egypt and the things you told me happened — even down to my divorce case last month!"

"Well, then, you believe in the study now, I suppose?"

"Oh, no, I don't. I cannot believe in such things; but there is money in it, my friend. You ought to make a fortune. Are you doing it now? I want some friends to see you."

"No, I am doing nothing, except some writing for the papers."

"Writing is for fools," the man laughed, and before Louis could collect his thoughts, he already had a glittering proposition placed before him.

The man was a government official with many extra curricular activities for making money, in fact by anything he could lay his hands on. Half an hour later, Louis emerged from the man's office with a sizable advance payment and a contract which bound him to begin hand-reading at once in London and to share on a fifty-fifty basis with his new Jewish partner, all the money he made for the next twelve years. His problem had been decided, his next step already taken. The world suddenly looked a very different place.

First he had to find suitable rooms in London's West End. The study of the hand was in disrepute and he received many refusals as a prospective tenant and many lectures on his choice of occupation. A Scots Roman Catholic was his first landlady who compromised with her religious scruples to allow him to stay, by doubling the rent. She sprinkled liberal quantities of holy water in the house both night and day and when he left a month later for larger premises, she charged him heavily for damage to her carpet — showing a quite proper sense of the relation between the religious and the practical.

Then there was the difficulty of deciding on his professional name. His Jewish partner suggested several biblical names, including Solomon. But this had unpleasant associations for him, having been applied to him in a recent divorce case and was rejected as asking for trouble, given that the candidate for its splendor was still a very young man.

They also delved into Shakespeare in their search for a suitable appellation but couldn't agree on any of the hundreds of names that came under consideration. Finally, Louis dreamt of seeing — in Greek and English — the word "Cheir", signifying hand, and determined in spite of his partner's opposition to adopt the name "Cheiro".

His brass plate was not in position an hour before it attracted the notice of a distinguished scholar. This first client complimented the young palmist on his perception and diagnosis and, without protest, gave impressions of his hands, signing them "A.J.B." He was Arthur James Balfour, President of the Society for Psychical Research, later to become Prime Minister and, as Lord Balfour, an envoy between Britain and the United States in connection with the settlement of the War Debt.

At a dinner party that night, Balfour related his interview, with the result that the next day Cheiro's rooms were besieged by clients. From this time, he was overwhelmed with work as a palmist and by the end of the first month his partner received back the money he had advanced, together with the 50 percent he had bargained for. He was extremely happy about his minor 'occult investment.'

However, his partner became frightened over the possibility of an old Act of Parliament on the illegality of such professions being invoked, the government official side of him taking over. He feared losing the pension that would shortly accrue to him and having received back his initial outlay plus a share of the profits, he was anxious to tear up the contract and sever all connection with his new source of income.

"Tear up the contract and burn it! And if you get into trouble never mention my name or that you even knew me!" The contract was burnt, they shook hands, and Louis was a free man once again.

More and more people came to hear what he could tell them. He became the rage of London society and his vogue seemed likely to continue for as long as his then immense vitality could stand the strain. It was, even more than he then realized, a tremendous drain on his nervous system to continue day after day, hour after hour, to dismiss one tangled web he would reveal to one client, and then be empty, receptive and concentrated for the next.

One evening in 1892, Cheiro showed up at a party given by Blanche Roosevelt in honor of Oscar Wilde, who was celebrating the opening night of his play, *The Importance of Being Ernest.* Tall, dark and handsome, wearing a dark capecoat, all eyes were immediately drawn to the entrance, where the young mystic stood.

A large, red curtain was set up in the middle of the drawing room with two holes cut in it. While curious onlookers inquired as to its purpose, Miss Roosevelt, a prominent London socialite and the party's hostess, walked to the middle of the room and announced:

"Ladies and gentlemen, this is Cheiro, the famous palmist that all of London has been talking about. I have invited him to examine the hands of some of my guests through this curtain without revealing their faces to him; so please enjoy yourselves."

One by one, pairs of hand were presented to him, and in each case the owner walked away dumbfounded. Finally, a pair of rather chubby hands was thrust through the curtain and a voice asked: "Tell me, my friend, what do you see?"

"You are a man who is bent on self destruction. When you are at the height of your career you will be involved in a scandalous trial which will leave you in ruin, and you will die in poverty on foreign soil. These are the hands of a king, but of a king who will send himself into exile."

Because the gentleman in question was at the very peak of his profession, everyone laughed. But the laughter was soon cut short by the tall, rotund figure who abruptly jumped to his feet and cried, "Be quiet! Did you not hear what he said?" Without another word, Oscar Wilde turned and left the party. History records his plummet from fame and the scandalous trials that ended his career, and eventually, his life. And thus began the saga of the incredible Cheiro, one of the greatest seers and proponents of palmistry in modern history.

Shortly after his appearance at Blanche Roosevelt's party, a young girl of 16 came to him for a reading. She wandered in off Bond Street, a young woman out on her first shopping expedition, alone. The manservant gravely asked her to wait because she had no appointment. The room, with its few choice pieces of furniture, thick carpets, soft lights and faintly perfumed with flowers, wrapped around her like a caress, and in a moment, a tall, handsome young man was smiling down at her. She held out her little hands for him to examine, and he told her:

"You will be wedded and widowed before you are twenty and twice married. Your first husband will disappear under mysterious circumstances, and because of the laws which rule our divorce courts, it will be many years before you will be allowed to remarry.

"A long period of uncertainty about your husband's death will prevent you from marrying the man of your choice though you will meet him again and again in every far-off corner of the world over many years. Eventually you will marry him."

She replied: "You are the only other man I would want to marry, if, as you say, I am *Fated* to lose my first husband. Therefore, can't you try and make the second come off a bit sooner?"

"What do you mean?"

"Simply that I mean to have you for my second husband if I can't have you for my first."

He thanked her for the compliment, smiled the smile of a man sure of himself, and bowed her out the door. He would never forget those small beautiful hands. Thus was it that his future wife first met Cheiro, and it was not until a few years later, in the early years of the new (20th) century, after she was a young widow that she was seated in a New York restaurant with Countess von Svoboda, and exclaimed, "Why, there is Cheiro! I must speak to him!"

When he joined them, his surprise equaled her own. He was about to leave for England, where he was very much a social lion, for in that period his lecture tours and private consultations enjoyed phenomenal success.

Their next meeting, again years later, was equally dramatic and unexpected. After some eventful years she had spent in the United States and England, her health had broken and doctors sent her to a warm, dry climate. This she found in Egypt where she had numerous adventures culminating in a trek with a camel caravan across the Sahara.

Staying at a hotel in Cairo trying to regain Western habits after her long sojourn in the desert, she thought she saw a familiar figure seated at her favorite table in a secluded corner when she came down to dinner.

Cheiro recognized the gypsy-like form that approached him, burnt brown by the desert sun. But again, it was just a brief encounter before he once again quickly went on his way. A lot of things happened in the intervening years before *Fate* finally brought them together. Uncertain days and years in China, Russia and Paris were to pass, punctuated by unsatisfying, fleeting encounters for both of them, before their lives were joined and the little girl eventually became Countess Mena Hamon.

By the end of the year Cheiro's health gave warning signals that it would not endure the demands he put on it. He was also feeling imprisoned by the life he was forced to lead, chained to his chair by a succession of importunate, harassed seekers. So he accepted an unexpected American offer and set off for the United States, accompanied, of course, by his unfailing travelling companion, The Mummy's Hand!

This time his arrival was much publicized, and when he stepped off the ship in New York he was greeted by a group of skeptical reporters and challenged to identify an assortment of handprints of notable and notorious people of whose identity he was unaware. He quickly accepted the challenge. One after the other he correctly assessed the personality and occupation belonging to each of the impressions. When he came to the last print, he said: "Whoever this man is, whether he had murdered one or ten people is not the question; as he enters his 44th year he will be brought to trial and condemned to death, and yet, his hand shows he will not die in the electric chair but will spend the rest of his life in prison."

The impression turned out be none other than that of Dr. Meyer, notorious as *The Chicago Poisoner*. For years he systematically poisoned his wealthy patients after insuring them for considerable amounts of money. After a sensational trial he was sentenced to die by electrocution.

One day Cheiro received a message from Sing Sing Penitentiary stating that "the Dr.," as he was called by prison officials, wanted to see him. "Cheiro," he pleaded, "I have lost my third and final appeal. Do you still hold true to what you told the reporters — about my escaping the chair? For God's sake, tell me!"

He stood by his prediction and, at the last moment, the death sentence was commuted to life imprisonment.

The American tour was an immediate success. Cheiro was able to move about more than before and found the atmosphere stimulating, more sincere, even if a tad naïve. He came through the grueling newspaper test of his powers with flying colors, which again netted him sensational publicity.

Cheiro's pronouncements were startling and accurate. He traveled throughout the continent touching New York, Chicago, Washington and Florida, and paused at various centres for a protracted stay where he varied his private consultations with his lectures. The young seer was now preceded by an agent and accompanied by an entourage: his secretary, business manager, the latter's wife (who had been a concert singer) and a Hindu servant.

By the time he got back to London, his health was restored and he repeated his former success. He did consultations for people from all ranks and from all walks of life: the famous, the great, and the not so great. Royalty, such as King Edward VII, the Czar of Russia, King Humbert of Italy, the Shah of Persia; notables like Pope Leo XIII, Lord Kitchener, British Prime Minister William Gladstone, Stanley (of "Dr. Livingstone, I presume?" fame), Cecil Rhodes, Chief Justice Shackleton, Lord Russell of Killowen, Marshall Hall, Lillie Langtry, and a whole bevy from the literary and artistic world including Oscar Wilde, Mark Twain, Sarah Bernhardt — and thousands more.

More than once, he assisted Scotland Yard in apprehending — what was until then — a completely unsuspected person, which he deduced from clues including bloodstained fingerprints left at the scene of a crime.

He always found the Achilles' heel of the celebrated and the respectable, but never revealed, or took advantage of it. Louis' clients knew they could trust him. The London of those days had, perhaps, a greater variety of characters than today. There was more poverty, but there were also more ostentatious displays of opulence and elegance in the style of the late Victorian era. The class system was very much in force, with much license allowed to those admitted to the tightly knit group that was called High Society.

During Britain's thriving commercial peak, the more enterprizing sons and some daughters of the best people could disappear on adventurous missions for a few months or even a year or two, and return to take up where they left off their place in the urbane, well-dressed, well-fed throng. Eccentricity was welcomed as adding excitement and variety to the pageantry of the social merry-go-round. People worked hard and long and played the same way. A healthy curiosity about the unknown was smiled upon and High Society dabbled, half-doubting, half believing, in all sorts of curiosities amongst which ghosts and spirit manifestations occupied a fair share of attention.

Into this sunny, leisurely, sometimes courtly milieu, Louis settled with the ease of a duck to water and was admired and sought after by rich and well-bred society beauties. As a presentable, unattached man with an unusual gift, he was in demand for dinner and house parties. Charming and gracious as he was, he knew his value and jealously protected his bachelor status. Some of his newly formed associations helped him still further into the lofty, inner circles. He became a Mason and belonged to the same Lodge, which numbered royalty among its members. When he went to Rome he was received by the Pope and permitted access to the priceless and unique wonders of the Vatican library.

So many opportunities of such varied kinds both social and for research in his chosen field were thrust upon him, that he had to make a choice between the superficial and the profound. Poverty and obscurity were his heritage, coupled with charm of manner, intuitive understanding and a special gift of interpretation — a gift he did not neglect. He said himself repeatedly that he obtained his success not only by inexplicable inspiration, but also by studying his subject as a science and by sheer hard work. He had something to offer which High Society craved.

They begged for it like children, showering him with gifts and favors. It's no wonder that he forsook whole-hearted devotion to sour austerity, to dally in the dazzling, silken world that was opened up to him. All through his life, apart from those who merely sought enlightenment on their domestic problems, there were those, enthroned in the seats of political or artistic power, who came as supplicants, asking, "How long will my success last?" or, "Is this set-back temporary?" or, "When will my luck change?"

About this time, he observed that a double *HeadLine* appeared on his hand, denoting two distinct personalities: that of Cheiro, which he felt *Fate* had forced upon him, and that of Count Louis Hamon, the gentleman, the man of means and leisure, a descendant of princes, occupying his rightful place in High Society, that he always wanted. And the two personalities were always in conflict. Try as he might, especially in later years, the Count was always flung back onto the other self -- Cheiro.

In his early days as a professional palmist, he affected the Oscar Wilde style of dress. His rooms were a crowded, bizarre medley reminiscent of Indian bazaars. Every obvious thing was done to draw attention to the occult — fretwork stalactites, garish hangings, strange lighting effects, crystal balls, model hands on cushions, potent fumes of incense, everything shrieked — Mystery! But all this was soon altered.

He briefly became interested in the theatrical world, becoming associated with Wilson Barrett, famous for his production of *The Sign of the Cross*. Cheiro's innate sense of theatre and drama was made truer by practice, his tastes refined by contact with many people in high places. He learned with an inherited aptitude to be a courtier! His flair for the dramatic, theatrics and show business would eventually lead him to his final destination: Hollywood, California. But first, many more perilous adventures would make demands not only of his time, but also on his health and sometimes nearly on his life!

Chapter Five

Bizarre

Cheiro's life was a jumble of strange happenings, although some were not without their humorous side; humorous, that is, when looked back upon years later, but perplexing enough at the time. Bizarre! The kind of things where only one unusual occurrence in anybody's life would be more than enough, but for him it was a stunning kaleidoscope of flashing pictures, each succeeded by another one still more strange.

On the humorous side, there was the woman who determined, following Cheiro's prophecy of her marriage at 48, that he would pay, either with his life or with his hand, if the predicted husband did not materialize.

She was a very large American lady who bombarded him with letters, telegrams and threats as the final year approached and then began to dwindle away. She spent time and money presenting herself attractively in places where it might be supposed that husbands were to be found. Finally, in despair and rage, she sent Cheiro a telegram stating she would call on him at a certain hour of a particular day, all other males having eluded her. Below are samples of the bombardment to which he was subjected:

Murray Hill Hotel,
New York,
9th March 1894.

Young Man,
Since my unfortunate interview with you on March 2nd, my entire life has become unnerved and disquieted by thoughts and feelings that I cannot understand. Since my early twenties, no such thoughts and feelings have entered the quiet sanctuary of my life as those that rack and disquiet me now! My brain had become absorbed in that spiritual knowledge of "self" that sees in man its destroyer and its foe. I had therefore steeled myself against this common enemy of my sex and had risen superior to the hysterical emotions that for thousands of years have placed women in his power.

In an unguarded moment I went to you and you have ruined my peace of mind by the supposed reading of a marriage for me at the seasonable, if matured, age of 48. Young man, you have gone too far. I am not a woman whose feelings can easily be played with. My emotions, once aroused, can never be allayed. I am nearing 48 now, and if I find as I enter that year that no man appears on the horizon then, young man, woe unto you! For your hour is, indeed, come!

Three months after this, Cheiro left New York and went to live in the Hotel Brunswick in Boston. He hadn't been there a week before this letter arrived:

Murray Hill Hotel,
New York,
15th June, 1894.

Young Man,
If you imagine you have escaped me, you are mistaken. You have left New York for no other purpose than that of eluding me but I cannot be eluded. I am now one month past 48 and no man yet. To attract this creature I have gone in evening dress to theatres every night! I have paid 150 dollars for seats you, in England, call stalls but no man yet!

Two months later came the following notification.

Murray Hill Hotel,
New York
August 3rd, 1894.

Young Man,
Am now 48 and 3 months and still no man! I will wait one week more and if then I am still an unmarried lady, I will take the train to Boston and you can take your choice of two alternatives, either disgrace and ruin or marrying me yourself.

That week was probably the longest in his life. He thought about leaving Boston and go away but he didn't. Getting more anxious by the minute, he started studying his own hand for clues about what he should do.

Then the ultimatum arrived:

Young man. I am on board one o'clock train for Boston; expect me at six.

Many men would have accepted a marriage so easily arranged, but at that period of his life, Cheiro certainly did not. Six o'clock arrived. The clock struck! In the distance he heard the rustle of skirts coming down the long corridor. (In those days ladies wore silk petticoats; the more they wore and the more noise they made, the more 'swanky' they were.)

The door opened. Cheiro's heart nearly stopped. There she stood -- an enormous monument of fat! This was long before the Hollywood Cure had been invented. She looked all the more formidable on account of the hat she wore ... she had evidently bought all the cockatoo wings in New York.

And there was a smile on her face that stretched from ear to ear! A smile of triumph, he thought. Turning towards the landing, she very sweetly called:

"Robert, oh Robert, come in here at once."

A meek, diminutive looking man appeared on the threshold, from behind her billowing skirts.

"Young man," she roared at Cheiro. "Here is my fiancée. I met him this morning on the train. Your prediction came true, after all. We are to be married at once."

Fate had again been kind to Cheiro.

Travelling back from the United States, Cheiro reached Paris in time for the Great Exhibition of 1900. He had just taken an apartment in the Rue Clément Marot, off the Champs Elysées and while waiting to take possession, stayed at a central hotel so that he might enjoy a week's holiday sightseeing and visiting the museums and galleries. By this time he had taken expert tuition to perfect his command of Parisian and colloquial French.

The idyllic period was passing like a pleasant dream when suddenly, his peace was shattered by no less than a challenge to a duel! The entire episode came about quite innocently. At a table in the hotel restaurant sat a young man on holiday, good-looking and alone. At the next sat a beautiful woman guarded by a possessive Spanish husband. By some coincidence they seemed to approach their tables about the same time and, having little else to distract their attention, occasionally their casual glances met.

The husband took the clean-shaven young man for a hated American, victors of the Spanish-American War and as his glances grew more fierce, the lady's grew more tender. Thinking herself unobserved, she dropped a scrap of paper at the young seer's feet, on which she had written a few lines. The husband instantly demanded possession of the message. Cheiro, having no inkling of what the paper contained, curtly refused. To avoid a scene, they walked to the Palm Court, and on receiving another refusal to surrender the paper, the husband hissed and handed him a card:

"Be good enough to wait in the hotel tomorrow at nine when you will hear from me!"

When he got to his room, Cheiro discovered that the note from her was only a request for an appointment the next morning at ten in the reading room, the lady having read his books and recognized him from his photographs.

"Keep my secret," she begged at the end, and this Cheiro decided to do; though he hoped he would not be forced to fight a duel on such a flimsy pretext.

The next morning another Spanish Marquis, more fiery than the first, made his appearance. With a few insults to keep the matter hot, the hour and place were fixed; six o'clock the next morning at the Cascade in the Bois de Boulogne.

"And the weapons?"

"Smith & Wesson revolver," returned Cheiro promptly.

He was rather hard-put to choose a second. He had been in Paris barely a week and knew no one. Then he recalled that Alastair D'Oyley, the son of his old friend, the Marquis D'Oyley, was in Paris. He was elated at the speed and romance of the whole adventure.

"But why choose a revolver?" he asked.

Cheiro replied that it was the only weapon he knew well, having learned its use in America.

"Splendid!" said D'Oyley. "Let's go up to Gaston Renettes shooting galleries and give yourself a few hours of practice."

Using the American drop shot, Cheiro, to his own amazement, his friend's and the attendants, struck the heart of the figure five times out of six with his bullets. They were talking in English and discussing the coming duel quite freely, and although Cheiro noticed one of the attendants seemed a little too interested, he thought no more about it and he and Alastair went off to lunch and spent the rest of the day in fairly high spirits. These evaporated by nightfall, however, and, preparations made, Cheiro had a poor night....

Alastair arrived at five o'clock the next morning. They drank some coffee in the chilly dawn and drove off through the woods to the meeting place. The beauty of spring morning passed quite unnoticed as one might expect, since Cheiro was certain he was being driven to his execution. But he hadn't the moral courage or the physical cowardice to back down. He observed, with misgiving that his opponents were already there, pacing impatiently up and down.

They bowed. The second was presented and he politely asked for a few words apart. A rather frantic discussion ensued, leading Cheiro to believe they were going to settle their differences without calling on him.

"Then they came towards me, the Spaniard looking as grave as if his mother-in-law had shown up at the wrong moment. Alastair was grinning from ear to ear.

'Well, my friend," he said, "you can keep your Smith & Wesson for another day. The Marquis' friend has funked it; he won't fight, but sends his apologies to you instead and trusts that your early rising will not upset your appetite for breakfast."

"But what has happened?" Cheiro asked.

"That I cannot make out," Alastair replied, "except that the man who challenged you sent this gentleman to say that the whole thing was a mistake on his part, that he had no right to demand satisfaction, and offers you a complete apology for having done so."

It was over a month before Cheiro solved the mystery, and then it was cleared up only by the lady herself. She came to see him to have her hands read once he was established in Paris.

The old proverb should be: 'Where there's a will there's a woman!' For in the end a woman always does what she wants, even if twenty jealous husbands stand in the way. The reason the duel fell through was a very simple one. The attendant at Gaston Renettes was the brother of her husband's valet, and he heard about the foreigner who was to fight a duel in the morning and the same foreigner whose revolver had hit the heart in the life-sized target five times out of six.

It's just as well that Cheiro avoided the invitation to take Solomon as his professional name. For he disclosed to so many ladies his awareness of their secrets and, in turn, was told so many more that it was inevitable that he would arouse the wrath of the men they shared them with, should it come to their knowledge that the secret was out.

An almost superhuman reserve and discretion were forced upon him, yet strangely enough when he was called to task, this was one of the few times when he was completely blameless

Cheiro had become friendly with Edward Marshall Hall following an appearance in court where he was called as a witness in a case and cross-examined by the great counsel, worthily acquitting himself. Having announced in the press that he was sailing in September for the United States on a lecture tour, Cheiro received a citation as correspondent in a divorce case and immediately turned to Marshall Hall for help.

In spite of Hall's friendly disbelief, Cheiro stuck to his story that he was completely innocent (in this case). The lady had been a persistent caller and an esteemed acquaintance. Nothing more. He was advised to postpone his departure, to put the affair in the hands of reputable solicitors and not to worry too much while he went off on his holiday.

This lady obviously had pursued him, written him love letters which, conveniently, were stolen from him and she recorded her feelings in her diary. All this, along with frequent visits and an apparently compromising episode with a veiled lady whose identify was suspected at a fancy dress ball at Covent Garden, made things look very bad for him.

Cheiro insisted that the veiled lady was unknown to him but the other side was emphatic that she was the woman in question. There was other evidence and so it was a very worried young palmist who went to Boulonge-sur-Mer -- but failed to relax. When he was there previously he rescued a drowning woman, identified by watching detectives as the respondent, and was duly photographed by them in the arms of her rescuer. This was to be *Fate's* last assault against him on this occasion. Cheiro recognized the woman he had rescued as the veiled woman from Covent Garden he had been unable to trace — and whose very existence his persecutors had doubted. The detective's photograph proved it. The petitioner withdrew the charges, apologized and paid all costs. Cheiro set sail for the United States in September after all.

While Cheiro was in New York, one Saturday evening a very determined man sought an interview saying it was of the greatest importance. Thinking he might be in trouble and in need of help, Cheiro pushed aside the proofs he was correcting of his first book, a manual on the study of the hand. He went over to his gaslit consulting table and asked his secretary to admit his unexpected visitor. It was a hot summer's night, and the door of the consulting room was open.

"That lands out on the stairs, does it not?" were the only words the caller spoke. Cheiro followed his usual practice of examining the left hand first. Finding his right hand free, the man slipped it into the breast of his coat.

Before Cheiro had time to speak the man pulled out his hand and lunged at his heart with a long, pointed dagger! Fortunately it struck a heavy cigarette case recently presented to him by Mme. Nordice, the celebrated prima donna. But as Cheiro reached for a small pistol, which he had just persuaded a suicidal client to leave with him, his assailant struck another blow which pierced his side! He grabbed the revolver and fired! The would-be assassin sprang away cursing and bolted down the stairs to Fifth Avenue.

A doctor was called and the wound, not serious, was stitched up. The noise attracted attention and the papers made a sensation of the incident. As a result, Cheiro received hundreds of letters from unknown friends in the American public. However, some accused him of organizing the whole thing as a publicity stunt. This unsavory publicity was bought at the expense of a scar that he bore his whole life.

A year later, a priest presented himself saying he had come to talk about that mysterious affair. Finding that Cheiro bore no rancor, he said the man's enmity had been caused by a prediction given some time ago to a young woman. After an unfortunate childhood, Cheiro told her she came under the influence of a man who nearly destroyed her. However, in a certain month of her thirtieth year, she would have an opportunity of breaking with him. And if she took this chance, she would have every likelihood of making a success of her life.

She tried to make the break, but unfortunately mentioned that she was acting on Cheiro's advice. As a result, this madman decided to get rid of the interloper. "Now, he's dying," the priest said, "has repented of his act and sends me as his ambassador to beg your forgiveness." Cheiro went with the priest to his assailant's deathbed, and had the satisfaction of knowing that the man died at peace.

The woman, even then on the road to success, eventually married one of the wealthiest men in New York. Years later, while dining with her husband in a chic Parisian restaurant, she caught sight of Cheiro. As they were leaving, she called a waiter and sent over a quickly scribbled message: "I owe my life's success and happiness to you. May God bless you for it."

Chapter Six

Ghosts and Marvels

One day Cheiro received a badly written letter on cheap notepaper inquiring about his fee to go to Waltham Cross to read the hand of a child. Then another scratchy note came, accepting the figure and fixing the following Sunday for his visit. It was a fine, sunny day, and Cheiro set out more from curiosity than anything else. He was met by a brusque, roughly clad boor who led him down a long walk that ended at the doorway of a pathetic little hovel on the outskirts of a wood. Here, an elderly woman, uneducated, but hard and wily, took him to an attic. Cheiro was shocked by what he saw. Chained to a stool was an unkempt ragged little girl of about fourteen, utterly untrained and with speech that was almost unhuman!

The woman said she was unlike other children and very delicate, so it was not possible to let her out of the house. It was her hands he was called upon to read, and all the woman wanted to know was how long she was likely to live. After the child had been coaxed and threatened to let him see her hands, Cheiro realized that she was not living with her parents. She was the daughter of intellectual people, but her mentality was entirely undeveloped.

He demanded to know her history and frightened the old hag into telling him that she had once been a baby farmer and had been imprisoned for the suspicious deaths of infants in her care, and that she had been persuaded for an annual sum to take in this child as long as she didn't reside in London. So for the past 14 years she lived common-law in this hovel with the boorish man who was a notorious poacher. He detested children and she had no sympathy for them at all, so the little girl was pushed out of sight and spent most of her life in this garret!

Payment for the child's support ceased two years before. To the man, the child was an irritation, a needless expense - of less use than an animal. He was going to kill her and bury her body in the woods. Only a superstitious fear on the woman's part, caused by a dream, stopped him. She said the child was uncanny and had a presentiment that she would not live long anyhow. Having unexpectedly made some money (probably through robbery, Cheiro suspected), the woman decided to send for him and ask that question.

Cheiro felt *Destiny* had summoned him to rescue this child. These people were so trigger-tempered that he was forced to promise that he would not to go to the police, fearing immediate harm to the girl. The woman was willing to let Cheiro take her away, but the man wouldn't release her until the money that was due for her keep was paid. Cheiro persuaded the woman to keep the child safe for another week, promising them not only to pay the arrears but reward her for resisting the man's murderous plan.

He wanted to trace the whereabouts of the mother, but her identity was not known, because the child was handed over by a nurse through whom payments were received. Then the money stopped. And the nurse disappeared. Cheiro tried to find out if the girl had ever been admitted to a home for foundlings or another charitable institution, but without success. The week was nearly over and he was still puzzled as to what was best for the child, when he was consulted by a handsome widow in her mid-thirties.

In her hand, at the base of the little finger, Cheiro observed a peculiar knotted blue vein, the same kind he had seen somewhere on another hand. And as he wondered he asked his visitor if there were any questions she wanted to ask.

"Yes," she replied. "There is one. You were quite right in saying I had a child when I was seventeen, I was unmarried and my child was taken away from me to save my name. A year later my family arranged a marriage with a man I barely knew, and I went to live with him in South Africa. After his death I returned to England and then, fourteen years later, I learned that the child was still alive, and up until two years ago was being supported by money from my father. But he died and I could not find any trace of my little one. Look at my hand again and for God's sake tell me if there is still hope!"

As he obeyed, Cheiro remembered where he had seen that peculiar blue knotted vein mark before. It was on the hand of that abandoned waif now awaiting sentence of death or liberation into a wider world. And here was the mother, who only asked to be able to lead her gently back into humanity. Thanks to Cheiro, mother and daughter were reunited, bringing this intrigue to a close.

Next is the horrifying, pitiful story of a dual personality, part man, part woman, and its tragic denouement. Cheiro was consulted by Sir William Standish, a reserved, short man with very small hands and feet and very gentle manners. He was the son of a rich, eccentric father and had inherited a great fortune, curiously willed so that large sums would be spent annually on charities. He was quite happy in its administration, well known as a self-effacing philanthropist and lived quietly with his wife and son. He and his wife had agreed, after the birth of the child, to live together only as friends. They were on good terms and their lives followed the routine of their class, a routine to some extent, dictated and dominated by the servants, necessary for people of good family. Of these servants, pompous and didactic, Sir William was afraid, why, he did not know. He involuntarily took great care to be scrupulously conventional.

In his hand was a double line of head and Cheiro told him that he had two distinct sides to his life, one very feminine. He admitted this and seemed glad to unburden himself. He said there were times when he became restless and seemed compelled to leave his home and take up another life, although his mind then became a blank and he didn't know what happened during these intervals.

So in order not to upset the family, and to avoid giving misleading explanations, he told them he had to make frequent trips to Rome on business, but he was aware that part of these mysterious periods was spent at a small luxurious flat that he kept in London and where he lived alone — as a woman! He was frightened because the restless periods were growing more frequent, almost monthly, and on one occasion when he came to, seated in his own library in his own clothes — he was wearing a pair of woman's buttoned boots! He was desperately afraid he would give himself away, dreading the effect of the revelation on not only himself, but also his wife, son and, almost more than the others - the servants!

His extreme reserve and fear permitted him to seek no medical advice. He wasn't religious in the accepted sense and being without a confidant, talking about it all to Cheiro seemed to give him some relief. The situation seemed to improve somewhat but Cheiro could give the man only minimum attention as he was due to leave for America once again. When he returned he called at the house, and was welcomed by the wife and son who both regarded him as a family friend. The husband was away on one of his frequent trips to Rome. His wife indicated that she thought he had a vocation for a religious life and occasionally went to a retreat.

Worried about how he should act, Cheiro was pondering the matter, in the park, when he was hailed by an acquaintance, a poor and eccentric poet who lived mainly on fantasy, in a cottage in Richmond. He was jubilant that happiness had at last found him. A strangely attractive visitor had romantically shared his home for a few days, then suddenly disappeared. He was devastated when he lost track of her and then a month later, she unexpectedly returned with no explanations, and they resumed life together as soul mates, bound now by marriage as well as congeniality.

He bore Cheiro off to witness his good fortune and admire this eighth wonder of the world. Little by little, as the evening wore on, it dawned upon Cheiro that this quiet, reserved, almost sleep-walking woman in the obvious wig was none other than Sir William Standish. Cheiro himself was not recognized by Standish.

So Cheiro made an excuse to leave knowing that disaster could not be long delayed. The hardy, chimerical poet, who lived on dreams, would no doubt survive it but how would it affect Standish himself, his trusting wife and their high-spirited, highly strung, but apparently normal son?

The next day Cheiro called at their house, hoping against hope that he had been mistaken. But no, the father was away, and the boy was planning to surprise him by joining him in Rome. They had, of course, the address to which letters were to be forwarded.

After a commotion at the door, Cheiro's friend, the poet, suddenly thrust past the impeccable butler demanding his wife! He had just seen her enter this very house with her own latchkey! She had fled the embrace of her husband, who had become inflamed by the wine from the night before.

"Our first kiss," lamented the poet. "Where is she? Where have you taken her?"

Before explanations could even be attempted, dragging footsteps sounded outside ... a fumbling touch came on the handle, and the door slowly opened.... Sir William Standish stood on the threshold, bedraggled and unkempt, still wearing woman's clothes. His wide open, entranced eyes stared at each of them in turn and they, with varying reactions, looked back at him. At last he made a supreme effort, and recognition dawned in his eyes. He staggered a step or two forward, cried "My wife! — my wife!" and fell lifeless at her feet.

On another evening in Cheiro's life there was more than a touch of the macabre when a well-dressed but distraught man sought him out late one evening with a plausible tale of some urgency and begged him as a matter of life and death, to go with him immediately to a waiting cab, to ask no questions, and to read someone's hands. "It is of terrible importance to me," the man stammered.

With some misgivings Cheiro complied - thinking that someone was ill, perhaps dying and that what he would reveal was obviously vital to this man's peace of mind, and perhaps also to the other person. In the cab, Cheiro was threatened with a revolver and blindfolded. It was a long drive, but all through it he sensed a continuance of high tension in the man at his side. At last they reached their destination. He was guided into what felt like a large, well-appointed house and led upstairs to a bedroom where the bandage was taken from his eyes. He took in the large room, richly hung and furnished, darkened by heavy curtains that draped the windows and illuminated only by a ray of moonlight.

On the bed lay a beautiful young woman, a sad expression on her face, and on her breast, an ebony crucifix. But the crucifix neither rose nor fell, for there was no breathing to cause it to do so. She was dead! Cheiro had been called upon to read the hands of a corpse! The companion of his journey brought another lamp, setting in on the coffin. The brass plate read: "Agnes Morton, age 24."

Reluctant at first, Cheiro felt compelled by an unseen power to read the hands and fearlessly tell what he saw. He told of a life filled with trouble and anxiety but redeemed by the great love she bore her husband. Since her early years, he went on, she had nourished a secret affection for someone she had cherished and helped with financial support. It was a relative, he was sure.

On hearing this, the man let out a great cry and collapsed. Cheiro released the dead hands at once and rushed to his side. On his recovery the man seemed bewildered, then nervously led Cheiro from the room, saying: "I have heard enough — all that I want to hear! Go, sir, for God's sake — leave me! Someday, perhaps, I will send for you and tell you all."

It was eight months before Cheiro was summoned to a private hotel near Charing Cross Station and was received by a coughing invalid who did not seem long for this world. Yet the voice was familiar and gradually he unfolded the tragic story of the events leading up to the dramatic and puzzling incident in which Cheiro read the hands of the dead girl.

"I was forty years of age, returning from active service in India, when I first met a beautiful girl of twenty who became my wife. She was travelling alone, except for her maid, and I soon realized there was some mystery about her life that she was anxious to conceal. When she agreed to marry me, it was only on condition that I never pry into the secret that caused her recurring fits of sadness.

"I only insisted on knowing that there was no lover in the background, and eagerly snatched my happiness, for we seemed equally dear to each other. When we reached England, we were married and lived an ideal life together for nearly three years. Then a letter came from India that upset her, but she refused to tell me anything about it. Unfortunately, instead of trying to earn her confidence by kindness, I became wildly jealous and decided she was false to me. I became determined to find out the truth and make her confess it. I stooped to all kinds of tricks: secretly watching her actions, bribing the postman so that I saw all incoming letters and finally I read a letter from her to someone who was in difficulties in India, to whom she was sending money and whom she addressed as 'My dearest boy.'

"One is insane when one is jealous. I made up my mind to commit suicide, first leaving all my property to her to 'make up for the three years she had waited for happiness,' and writing a heartbroken letter to tell her I had discovered her treachery, but that by the dawn of another day she would be free to return to India to marry the man she loved.

"While I was doing this, I heard her moving about in her room. 'She cannot sleep,' I thought, 'perhaps she had one of her attacks of neuralgia. But she will have rest when I am dead.' Her door opened, she came to my door and knocked.

"She said she was in agony and asked me for some laudanum to ease the pain. She saw the open medicine chest and feared I was ill, asking my forgiveness for her recent absorption in her own affairs and withdrawal from me. I could not trust myself to speak, 'but in the morning,' I thought, 'my letter will speak for me.' I pushed her from me roughly in my anxiety to cut short a painful interview, quickly handed her a small bottle and resumed my seat at my desk.

"Slowly and reluctantly she went toward the door, paused a moment on the threshold, and our eyes met. She said 'Goodnight.' I said 'Goodbye'.

"Troubled and disturbed, I resumed my letter. I did not like what I had written. It seemed too harsh so I tore it up and began another. I did this again and again until I was surprised to find the day breaking and my deed not done. 'After all,' I thought, 'a few lines will do,' so I hastily wrote: 'Goodbye! I have discovered all. You are now free. May you be happy!'

"I made a few other preparations and then, thinking she would be asleep, allowed myself once more, for the last time, to gaze on that face I had loved so much. I stole into her room. She lay motionless in the half-light of dawn. I brushed back my tears so as not to waken her and bent down for one last kiss. Her lips were icy. A shaft of fear shot through me! I tore back the bedclothes and pressed her to my heart. I kissed her hands, her face, her breast.... She was dead!

"In my excitement I had given her — instead of laudanum — the poison I intended to take myself! The only point I cannot explain is my going for you on that awful night and getting you to read those dead hands. It was well I did so. You said that "someone she loved, a relative, had been a burden on her and ruined her life." You were right. The man was her own brother, who had fled England in disgrace. I have lived only to carry out her wishes in regard to him. I have been to India. I have seen him there. Now I have returned, to die."

Three weeks later, Cheiro was the sole mourner who followed to the grave, the remains of Colonel Morton....

Another bizarre event unfolded in London when Jehangiar Colan, a young Parsee, who afterwards became Cheiro's secretary, introduced the Seer to the strange Hampstead recluse, Elmond Savroy Diodiardi, Duc le Ravigo.

Challenged to demonstrate his abilities, Cheiro's statements were later more aptly confirmed by his host. A singularly gifted man, at thirteen Ravigo shared with Gunoud the gold medal for music given by the Paris Conservatoire. Later he became a noted French advocate, who chivalrously went to the rescue of a sailor wrongly accused of mutiny and suffering on Devil's Island, because the lad's mother had once befriended him. At thirty, after the woman he loved died, he gave up on the material world and entered a monastery, undergoing long years of study and emerging only to fulfill some great purpose.

Satisfied of Cheiro's bona fides, the recluse disclosed his name and his intention of sharing his problems and the solution with his new friend. His aim was to bring back the dead from the Great Beyond. Already, with the aid of his wonderful music, he had accomplished much. But his other concepts were even more daring, almost justified by his experiments in medical application of electricity, which had, from time to time, achieved what then seemed miraculous cures. There is no doubt that he was far ahead of his time and had accomplished many things that other men considered impossible, so that even his most fantastic projects demanded a certain credence.

This was the man who had developed the Thought Machine, an extremely sensitive register of emotions and conditions of mind. "It showed whether a person had will-power or concentration, or the reverse. And one of the most remarkable things about it was that it instantaneously registered the effect of drugs or alcohol on the effort of thought." William Gladstone, then England's Prime Minister was among the distinguished people who gave it exhaustive tests. When it was tested on Cheiro, it recorded in him an immense degree of concentration.

The final experiment shared by this recluse and Cheiro was when the machine was used — in pre-radio days — as a human receiver in a wireless apparatus which was intended to unroll the scroll of time, as well as space.

The receiver was required to lie on a glass-insulated copper couch, arranged north to south, pinioned by a copper helmet and copper bands terminating in a 12-pointed magnet. Other wires connected with an aerial, a magnifier and an earth (a zinc rod at the bottom of a well in the garden). The recluse then wandered off into the grand cadences of his organ music and Cheiro experienced an extraordinary, awe-inspiring vision of lost Atlantis, in its prime, and another one at the dreadful moment of its passing.

Two other incidents indicate the influence of heredity — one tailing off into crime and depravity — but both portraying brilliant members of humanity, seemingly born under an unlucky star and doomed to failure and disappointment.

The first incident began when Blanche Roosevelt, a beautiful young girl of sixteen, sailed with her mother from

New York to begin training in Milan for an operatic career. An American millionaire, Major Alexander Davis, a notable collector of precious stones, chanced to be on the same ship. Had she been a jewel, he doubtless would have bought Blanche for his collection. She was a young girl with an old fashioned mother and he an older, unhappily married man with a family, so that such a transaction, however veiled, was impossible. However, he foresaw the difficulties ahead of her and contented himself with giving her his card, on which was written: "If at any time you get into trouble, contact me and I will come to your assistance."

When she was eighteen, her beauty was the talk of the town and she was considered ready to make her debut as Juliet at the Milan Opera House. That afternoon, at the Jockey Club, Prince Maro di Colonna toasted her coming success as Juliet, and Count Machetta toasted his success with her as a real life Romeo. The two men quarrelled, the Count betting on his triumph in the second role after hers in the first. His proof would consist in dropping his boots from her bedroom window.

There was no doubt of her success. The enthusiastic crowd, smothering her with flowers, unharnessed the horses of her carriage and drew her back in triumph to her hotel. Meanwhile the Count, hours before, had hidden himself on her balcony from which after an appropriate interval, he threw down his boots, then climbed down to join his waiting friends and claim his reward.

Although completely innocent, the ensuing scandal became so great that Blanche's operatic career was ruined and the Count was forced to make her his bride. The unhappy union was blessed by the Church and the Cardinal of Milan performed the ceremony. It could only be dissolved by death. Eventually, Blanche left her husband and sought escape in the artistic circles of Paris and London. Her novel, *The Copper Queen* with its vivid picture of the Chicago fire, attracted encouragement from Bulwer Lytton and others. She was always volatile, however, and eventually drifted away from writing. When her mother died, she lost the anchor that had fitfully bound her to proper conduct. Her fatal beauty and vivacity were exploited by a series of adventurer-type men. The excitement of gambling, drinking and drugs sustained her, and her debts continued to mount up — many times paid off by her never-failing friend, Major Davis.

Deciding that London was the safest place for her to live, he finally settled on an income to be paid to her monthly, providing she never to return to Paris or Monte Carlo. For two years she prospered, occupying a handsome suite at the Savoy Hotel and establishing a brilliant salon which attracted the most celebrated artists, writers, and musicians of the period.

She then became friendly with a wealthy American, Sir Richard Musgrave, who had inherited an estate in the north of England, which carried with it a title. He married her companion and made his rich mansion, facing Hyde Park, into an elaborate gaming hall where wine and money flowed freely. It was under police observation when a young man, complaining he'd been cheated, was brutally murdered there, his head cloven through with a cutlass. The visitors in a panic managed to escape by various exits, and the only clue left for the police after the mêlée was a woman's blue ostrich feather fan. This had been given to Blanche the previous Christmas by Cheiro.

Blanche slipped away to Paris and plunging back into a life of dissipation to forget this grisly incident. *Luck* seemed to have deserted her in Paris, and again at Monte Carlo. But once more Major Davis came to her rescue. He established her this time in a big old house off Portman Square in London's fashionable West End, which she furnished and decorated exquisitely. At the housewarming party she assured Cheiro that, warned by her many disasters, and frightened by the *Fate* that befell Sir Richard Musgrave — who fled England only to be arrested in New York and sentenced to life imprisonment in Sing Sing — she was determined never to gamble again but to live peacefully in London until her end came. "You have always predicted my years would not be long. Perhaps this is the haven you promised me where the storms of life could not enter."

The fright regarding the murder calmed a little as each day succeeded the next, without the murderer's discovery or even any further mention of the crime. But no more than a week later, Blanche was resting on a divan, her heart not being very strong, idly glancing through the newspapers. There was nothing of special interest for her, until the front page of the last paper. There she saw in bold type: "THE CUTLASS CASE! Scotland Yard has discovered the owner of the ostrich fan."

She fell back in a state of collapse, passing into a coma from which she never recovered. Faithful as ever, Major Davis came forward to do one last service, erecting on her tomb in Brompton Cemetery, a life-size statue of her in white marble, a beautiful figure of an angel, a goddess, his last tribute to the Blanche that might have been.

London is also where Cheiro became part of the bizarre story of the princess and the lion tamer. Princess de Montgly moved, as if by right, in exalted circles. Later, it was through the ill-starred Princess that Cheiro met King Edward VII, when he was the Prince of Wales.

Her mother, Countess de mercy Argenteau and Princess de Montylong, was one of the beautiful throng of ladies-in-waiting to the Empress Eugenie, and was a particular favorite with Napoleon III. Eight years before his downfall, the Countess' only child was born, an event celebrated with great magnificence; the Emperor himself standing godfather to the little Princess.

With great difficulty and personal danger, her mother later managed to visit the Emperor during his captivity in Germany, and then in a meeting with the King of Prussia and Chancellor Bismarck, at Versailles, to alleviate the treatment to be meted out to the vanquished Emperor. Failing in her desire to be of assistance to her Emperor, she retired to the Chateau d'argenteau in Belgium and remained there until her death.

It was here that the Princess, who initially disappointed her mother by not being a boy, spent her lonely childhood. Growing up beautiful, at eighteen she married the Duc d'Avaray, a marriage arranged by her mother. For some years, in Paris and London, she was the queen of High Society. The Prince of Wales was one of her admirers and he attended most of her sparkling receptions.

But her marriage was unhappy, embittered by the jealousy and enmity of another woman. She finally left her husband and returned to her ancestral chateau, living quietly, but in magnificence, surrounded by her dogs and the wonderful peacocks which were a feature of the estate.

Here, one particularly wintry Christmastide, Cheiro found himself the only member of a house party that had braved the storm and heavy snowfall. For nearly a week they were snowbound. Their first visitors were the King of Belgium and his daughter, Princess Clementine, who arrived by sleigh.

They were all quite happily marooned until an escort could arrive from the Palace at Laeken to shepherd them back.

But one evening as the storm raged outside, the small group passed the time by accepting hand-readings from Cheiro who also demonstrated his rarely used hypnotizing abilities:

"I really am impressed by your predictive skills as a seer, Cheiro, but I really don't think I believe in such things as mesmerism," declared Princess Clemantine.

And with that, Cheiro accepted the challenge: "Would you allow me to mesmerize you, your highness?"

She promptly agreed, and as Cheiro asked her to recline on a chaise lounge, in front of the fireplace, the gaslights were turned down, creating in the heavily draped and densely furnished Victorian drawing-room, an eerie atmosphere as the whiteness of the driving snow pelted against the great paned windows.

After a series of soft, soothing, often repeated suggestions to the Princess saying: "relax...deeply.... — as though you are sinking right through this place on which you are resting, because your body has become too heavy...", Cheiro gave a post-hypnotic command: "At the stroke of midnight you will rise from your bed and come directly to my quarters, after everyone else is asleep. But, now, when I count to three and clap my hands, you will awaken and remember nothing."

At the clap, she abruptly opened her eyes and laughingly said, "I knew you couldn't do it, my will is too strong for you." Hours later, when everyone had retired, Cheiro awoke to find the Princess standing in her silken white nightgown at the entrance to his quarters, the door flung wide open. It was exactly midnight. Of course he immediately sent her back to her rooms. (Or at least, that's what he said he did.)

Cheiro had foretold that a financial crisis and dramatic romance in the New World lay ahead for Princess de Montglyon. After numerous extravagances, all the family heirlooms, including the chateau and its peacocks, were swept away to pay her debts. She returned to Paris and there happened to see Bonavita, a fearless American lion-tamer, at the Moulin Rouge. He was a man of splendid physique and renowned as the one lion-tamer who never used a whip.

When she attended one of his performances, all the beasts, except one, obeyed his nonchalant commands. But one lion knocked down the fearless trainer and savaged his right arm and shoulder. With great courage, the Princess rushed forward and assisted in protecting the injured man and helped carry him to safety. She went with him to the hospital where an operation saved his life, but not his arm. (After this he was called Lefty).

When he was well enough to leave for America, she accompanied him, telling Cheiro, "Bonavita is not strong enough to travel alone."

A month later, he received a letter from New York: "You can announce to your friends — don't trouble about mine, I have none now — that Princess de Montglyon has married Bonavita, the lion-tamer. I may have lost a great deal in my life, but I have, in the end, found love."

Two years later, the epilogue was written:

"Bonavita was the best and noblest man I ever met, she wrote, "but his ways were not my ways, nor my ways his. We have separated forever. I shall remain in America. But alone."

Chapter Seven

Gold Rush and Fools Gold

Now that he was a man of means with considerable capital piling up behind him, in spite of the heavy expenses incurred by his constant travelling and lavish style of living, Cheiro resolved not to concentrate exclusively on hand reading and looked about for other suitable enterprises to invest in.

Some of his capital had come to him in the form of gold dust or nuggets when he happened to be in the United States during the Klondike Gold Rush days that swept like a fever through the country.

Infected by the prevailing craze, he even joined the general exodus but stopped enroute to observe the maelstrom of would-be diggers gathering their equipment. He found it far more profitable to linger in Seattle in awe of this phenomenon, where most of the gold seekers gathered before heading north to Alaska and Canada, and forecast for them their likelihood of striking it rich.

After leaving Seattle, Cheiro went to Chicago, a city always engaged in bustle and big business that he found intensely stimulating. He met a man, who claimed, with a reasonable degree of tangible evidence to prove it, that he could make gold! He was having dinner in the Auditorium Hotel one evening when he looked up to see a very strange individual observing him. Accustomed to forming rapid impressions of the many people he met, and acting on them, Cheiro quickly sensed an inborn courtesy and refinement in his visitor, despite his shaggy lion's mane and rough appearance. He invited the stranger to share his meal.

He proved to be a Metis, half French-Canadian and half-native, of the Sioux tribe, named Henri Dupont, a companion of Louis Riel, who fought against the English and was later hanged by them. Dupont had been taken prisoner and sentenced to death, but escaped by swimming across the St. Lawrence River from Canada to the United States, handicapped by a bullet wound in the shoulder, a parting gift from a watchful sentry. Outlawed by Canada, he settled in the United States which he liked much better. But he was a natural rebel and idealist and burned to remedy the many injustices perpetrated against natives.

He was particularly bitter about racial cruelty and oppression inflicted by the white man on the colored races. He had a marvelous plan to change all this and build a worldwide Utopia on earth. "But how can it be carried out?" Cheiro asked, spellbound by the rush of words and ideas.

"Through the possession of unlimited wealth," he answered, "utilized as God intended wealth to be used."

"But where is this wealth to come from?" Cheiro inquired. "It increases only in the hands of those who have it. Remember the very hard but true to life biblical text which says: 'Unto him that hath shall be given, but from him that hath not, shall be taken away even that which he hath.' "

The answer was that a friend of his, a young American chemist had discovered how *Nature* formed metals and jewels and he claimed he could repeat the process. His laboratory and plant lay on the outskirts of Chicago itself and Dupont asked Cheiro to accompany him there to meet this scientist. Skeptical but receptive, Cheiro agreed to go. An hour's drive brought them to a large building, part brick, part galvanized iron, standing alone in a dreary, frozen field. Dupont's key admitted them by a side door and they made their way through ill-lit passages to a large central room.

Here, a young man was seated at a long table littered with microscopes and instruments, intent on the examination of a clay-like substance. Dupont vouched for their visitor, who was greeted by the young scientist. At last Cheiro realized Dupont's purpose in seeking him out and bringing them together. He wanted him to read the young man's hands to see if success would crown their efforts.

The chemist was far from being a charlatan. His first aim had been, while still an assistant, to save enough money to enable him to study every well-known volcano in the world. He had put aside other temptations and devoted his energy and ability to testing his theories personally, by such experiments as his being let down into Mount Vesuvius by a steel rope! By discovering and applying these natural laws to heat and the affinities of clays and metals, he returned to New York and invented a furnace that would dissolve clay and sand so as to form bricks with a beautiful white stone effect. These bricks were in much demand commercially and he sold the entire process for a tidy sum. This provided him with the capital he needed to build the plant they were in, erected for the sole purpose of creating a rapid reproduction of the earth's natural method of making gold and precious stones.

Was he an imposter who had sacrificed a profitable brick factory for a will-o'-the-wisp scheme, the age-old dream of the alchemist? Was it a confidence trick? Or was he another Curie, his faith and success not yet acknowledged, who would confer untold wealth onto mankind? As the days passed and Cheiro learned more of his methods of reproducing gold and jewels and seeing them in crucibles with his own eyes, he started to believe. Hardheaded businessmen in Chicago took the same view to the extent that shares in the enterprise, first issued at twenty dollars, were now hard to get at $450 each.

It was on this foundation that Henri Dupont based his hopes of furthering his humanitarian plans. But the hands! On one side of the table sat Dupont, concentrated, eager, alert, a man with an idealistic purpose; on the other sat the chemist, pale and careworn by excessive heavy labor, mental effort and frustration. On the table lay the evidence: several glass jars of small rubies, a leather bag of small fine gold nuggets, worth $5,000.

The young chemist's hands revealed extraordinary brainpower but indicated no fortune to come by it. The two men were not depressed by this verdict. They were accustomed to the doubt of others and Cheiro's statement, made so reluctantly in view of their hopes, only caused them to doubt him. To offset their disappointment and indicate his goodwill, he asked to purchase a sizable quantity of shares in their enterprise, though this must have seemed to them a contradiction in view of what he had just told them.
Several times in the following six weeks he drove out to the factory in the evening to find everything progressing most satisfactorily and hopefully. The price of shares continued to rise and Cheiro almost regretted he hadn't bought more.

Then came a particularly cold wintry spell, the most severe Chicago had known in years. The snow was so deep that for almost two weeks he was weather-bound in his hotel. At this point he received a visit from an anxious Dupont. Production at the factory had almost ceased due to inability to get material from the frosted, snow-covered ground in Utah and transport it to the plant. He feared that should the newspapers learn of the stoppage, they would attribute it to other causes. With great difficulty, and to preserve appearances, one furnace was kept going.

No other earth and rock, easier to access, would give them the same results, Dupont explained, in answer to a suggestion from Cheiro. He then begged Cheiro to go out with him to the plant. They reached it and were joined by four other interested shareholders and held a council of war. The chemist, prostrated by this additional anxiety, was resting upstairs on the camp bed he reserved for those brief moments he permitted himself to rest.

Various alternative plans were discussed. To others their alarm might have seemed groundless because the same weather conditions affected all industry at that moment. But later, events proved their fears justified, and in more than one way. It was decided to keep the one furnace going to avoid, as long as possible, disclosing the situation to anyone, even their own families, in the hope that conditions would improve sufficiently to resume normal output — and especially that the present crisis not arouse negative publicity.

All the men offered to remain and sleep on the premises so that no one could be persuaded or bribed to give information. Similarly, the shareholders present remained loyal, not one share being sold, for they all realized that any sudden unloading of the shares might also provoke inquiry, and their downfall. There was still a good market at $450 a share, and many of them could have made a small fortune. During the week Cheiro received five offers for his shares, but turned them down.

By the end of the week the terrible frost showed no signs of breaking, and weather reports predicted it would probably hold for another two months. The inventor therefore decided to call a general meeting of shareholders at the factory on the coming Saturday evening. When the time arrived, so bitter was the cold that no more than fifty people assembled, and they all huddled round the open door of the single furnace that was running to keep warm.

The inventor explained the position, and he was followed by Dupont who confirmed his remarks and, in a fighting speech, asked for a vote of confidence and enough money to carry on until the frost broke and supplies could be resumed. Unfortunately the wilder element present got the upper hand -- howling their disapproval. The meeting dissolved in chaos. The inventor was threatened with personal violence, but Dupont not only shielded him with his body but also whipped out a revolver to control the unruly mob.

The chemist kept his head. He assured the others he was not a charlatan and asked for six volunteers to assist him. Before their eyes they would have a test done to see what could be produced. There was agreement to this proposal and Cheiro was one of the six men selected. Off they went to carry out their instructions, one to operate a machine which crushed the remaining Utah rock into powder, another to shovel a few buckets of local earth from under the snow, two others to stoke the furnace, Cheiro and one other man were to fill the crucibles. When everything was ready the crucibles were put into the furnace. There was complete silence.

The inventor stood, watch in hand, eyeing the thermometer, because his special system of draught regulation and concentrated heat enabled the required temperature to be very quickly reached. At a certain moment he ordered the crucibles to be withdrawn, white hot and so brilliant that it hurt the eyes to look at them without dark glasses. Then they underwent rapid cooling and, when opened, disclosed what seemed like solid masses of rock. Two shareholders broke them open and small clear veins of gold could be seen glittering under the powerful lamp. Everyone was amazed! The fragments were passed from hand to hand, examined, commented on and then the gold was dug out with penknives.

Half an hour passed. They were all still thrilled by the seeming miracle they had witnessed, when somebody happened to say, "Where is he?" They all looked around and then went through the works calling his name. They went into the camp where he slept. They searched everywhere but he was gone.

Dupont was heartbroken and mystified. It was not only the loss of material success and wealth but also the disappointment in a friend he had trusted and on whose genius he would have staked his life. Gone also was his dream of using that wealth to promote human brotherhood.

Gradually, as the night wore on, the others slipped away until at last only Cheiro and an old caretaker, who shuffled around turning off the lights, were left.

"Come back with me. It's no use staying here," Cheiro urged. Dupont went with him -- like a sleepwalker. Not a word was spoken on the cold, dreary drive. Cheiro begged him, when they reached the hotel, to go in, eat something, and rest. This seemed to rouse him, but he only said: "I must find my friend," wrung Cheiro's hand, and went off into the snow and the night.

Cheiro felt Dupont was genuine. He had honestly believed in the chemist's genius and his ability to produce untold wealth — wealth he desired not for himself, but to fulfill his idealistic purpose. Of the chemist he was not so sure. Why had he chosen that particular moment to disappear? Why had both of them been so frightened by this temporary stoppage and infected the others with their fear? If the gold and jewels had been surreptitiously introduced, much bait had already been expended without corresponding hauls of big fish. If, on the other hand, they were genuinely created by this process, why creep away when they had won back the hostile shareholders? And why had Dupont also gone? Was it to look for and comfort an idealistic friend, wounded by the suspicion of those who professed to be his friends? Or was it to make his own getaway, before the inevitable inquiry that he would have to face, if he remained? The mystery was never solved and he never saw either of them again.

The next day the Chicago newspapers were full of the story, and the shares, so recently hard to come by at $450 each, hurtled down until they were worth only 25 cents apiece, and then there were no buyers. The tumult and shouting died down, and the newspapers eventually found another sensation to lavish their exuberant energy on.

Chapter Eight

Backstage with Royalty in Europe

The new century opened hopefully for Cheiro. He was a handsome man in his early thirties, with good health and no encumbrances. He had made his way by dint of perseverance into a leisured world that he felt was his by right of his noble antecedents. Wherever he went, his arrival was hailed with excitement since he was widely acknowledged as the messenger of *Fate*, unlocking the pages of the future. He was fawned over and flattered, in the secret hope that his revelations about them would be favorably influenced. The few who dared to behave otherwise were frowned upon by the faithful many as showing ignorance and bad manners. But to them, too, Cheiro preserved his suavity and charm. Not for nothing had he profited by the advice of one of his boyhood mentors: "Do good to those who do good to you; and as for those who do you harm, be sorry for their lack of judgment. If you follow this rule, it may not make you a millionaire, but it will at least give you great satisfaction."

At times, it looked very much as if he might become a millionaire all the same. In America his door was constantly besieged, his fees high, and competition of would-be supplicants so keen that they regularly auctioned off the last appointment of the day between themselves to the highest bidder. He became well known across the country for his lecture tours, and he also gave regular evening class sessions to serious students of palmistry.

In London it was his honesty and urbane style — the truth delivered with a smile — plus a certain youthful ingenuousness and modesty that won over High Society's heart and made him it's darling. He enjoyed royal favor, hobnobbed with Kings and Princes, kept their secrets, revealed their *Fate* and was never once proved wrong. His humbler friends found him equally fascinating. Kings or shop assistants, potentates or servants, they all received the same grave, courteous attention and his employees repaid this with a rare loyalty, remaining in his service for many long years.

He created such a furor during his first season in London that the newspaper publicity was incredible, some flattering and some hostile. This was when the old Act of

Parliament against those practicing palmistry, astrology, witchcraft, or all such works of the devil, was brought up and questions were asked about him in the House of Commons. A polite police inspector called and informed him that no steps would be taken to enforce this old Parliamentary Act if he closed his office and consulting rooms by the end of the week. He fulfilled his standing engagements faithfully, but when one of the ladies who visited him asked him to demonstrate his gifts at an evening party at her house, he was forced to agree to do so on an honorary basis only, in view of the expiry day.

But one of the laughing skeptics at this assembly was Sir George Lewis, the noted criminal lawyer. On the position being explained to him, he sent Cheiro his card, saying, "You are working on such a totally different foundation from what this old Act was intended to apply to that you do not come under it. Send my card to Scotland Yard and tell them to address any further communications to me."

Cheiro complied with the instructions, resumed his professional life, and never again heard of any interference or talk regarding this Act of Parliament being applied to him.

In 1896, he made a hasty journey to Ireland from America to attend at the deathbed of his father. Even though his son was now so traveled and looked well and prosperous, the old man never quite forgave him for following an occupation that he despised and felt was beneath the family dignity.

Nevertheless he preserved a deep, though stiff-necked, affection for his son and earnestly tried, in his dying moments, to reveal to him a long-kept family secret, the whereabouts of certain deeds and papers that would be valuable to him. The name and address of the solicitors who held these documents, however, eluded his memory and though he remained conscious for some time and tried repeatedly to speak, paralysis had seized him and he died regretting that pride had not allowed him to pass on this knowledge when he had the power to do so, years before.

At the time, Cheiro thought little of the omission, since his eyes were on the future and he had no inclination to linger nostalgically on the glories of a past to which he never wanted to return.

His young sister also died, and his mother at first remained in Ireland but later made her home with him in London, until her death. But through all this he was as busy as ever, travelling back and forth during the next few years between America and England. One particular Sunday afternoon, about three years later, he was waiting at a railway station on the outskirts of London for some friends who were coming from the south. The train was delayed and he had to fill three hours. Looking around for something to occupy the time, he chanced to see an announcement in a spiritualist journal about a séance to be held that very afternoon in a house close to the station.

He went along, quite skeptical, but more with the idea of filling in the time, rather than anything else. He was kindly received and during the séance, led by the blind medium, Cecil Husk, the spirit of his father materialized. Still resisting what he saw, he refused to acknowledge it until his father pointed to a white scar on his own nose, caused by an accident.

The ghostly specter sent loving messages in the very accent and intonation of life, saying how happy he was at last to be able to give Cheiro the information he had been unable to impart on his deathbed. He told Cheiro the name of a long-forgotten solicitor's office, describing the building as being on the left-hand side of a narrow street, near a church off the Strand. According to the ghost, they still had the papers and he begged his son to go and retrieve them.

"Father, I will come here every night if only you would speak to me again," Cheiro pleaded.

"No, my son, I have done what I must. I will come to you again, someday, but take this as proof of the Great Beyond, such proof as I never knew... be grateful. For when one asks for too much, one often loses all. Goodbye, my son, goodbye...."

Early next morning Cheiro combed the Strand and discovered what he sought -- Holywell Street, close to St. Clement Danes Church. At first he could find no Davis & Son, solicitors but eventually he did and with patience and a five pound note, induced the old clerk to dig up the long buried papers which told him of his family's lost heritage which enabled him henceforth to assume the ancient name and title. This was later legalized by deed poll.

Travelling back from the United States, he reached Paris in time for the Great Exhibition of 1900. He settled in an apartment off the Champs Elysées and was soon just as much in demand with an international clientele, augmented by the influx of visitors to the Exhibition, as he had been in London and America. Cheiro enjoyed life in the beautiful French capital where he gathered many friends about him and spent many pleasant moments on the French Riviera. He entertained lavishly, and now and then tested the tables of Monte Carlo. He had considerable success, though he regarded his winnings dolefully, because achieving them involved hours of exhausting calculations.

While the Exhibition was still in full swing, he was invited to a luncheon given in honor of Senator Thomas Walsh, a wealthy American with extensive mining interests in Montana and one of the American Commissioners to Paris. The luncheon was held in the United States Pavilion and attended by an international assembly. Speeches were made by the American Ambassador, the Commissioner General and the President of the American Chamber of Commerce. Then, unexpectedly, the chairman called upon Cheiro for a few words.

As he rose, Leopold II, King of Belgium, a personal friend of Mr. Walsh, entered and stood at the door with his aide-de-camp, Count d'Outremont. Cheiro was taken by surprise but conducted himself so well that he was loudly applauded. The King demanded to be introduced to him, adding his congratulations on a feat he always envied - the power to meet an occasion with apt and ready speech. When they met later in the week at a reception given by Mr. Walsh, the King again singled him out, asking for his address — "perhaps in one of my leisure moments I may want to avail myself of your talents."

The King's condescension was remarked upon and Cheiro was the victim of the jealousy it aroused. Two days later, as he was sitting down to an early lunch, an elderly man, remarkably resembling the King of Belgium, was announced. Sure enough, it was he, and as Cheiro apologized for the smell of his lunch permeating the apartment, the King said: "Mons. Cheiro, I want you to do me a favor. I'm sure I smell Irish stew; it is a dish I have always relished, so please do me the favor of asking me to help you with it."

Brushing aside Cheiro's hesitation, the King gently admonished him not to let his favorite dish get cold. As Cheiro remarked afterwards: "Fortunately, the stew was really a good one, because my French cook happened to be an Irish woman married to a chef at the Café de Paris, and Irish stew was to her a kind of sacred memory of all that was best about her motherland. During the lunch the conversation centered mainly on the United States, whose modern developments and great variety of citizens Cheiro's occupation had enabled him to observe.

Adjourning after coffee and cigarettes to his consulting room, together they examined the King's long, intellectual hands. The royal visitor was so interested in what Cheiro told him, that it was four o'clock before he left, having exacted a promise that the reading should be resumed the following Saturday at Laeken Palace in Brussels.

Canceling his full list of appointments for the following two days, Cheiro arrived at a modernized chateau set in beautiful woodland, and presented to the guard the card the King had given him. It gained him instant admittance at the appointed hour. He found himself seated in what might well have been a plainly furnished hotel sitting room.

The King appeared, smoking his usual cigar, and led him, with the utmost informality, into his study; there was no mention of continuing the hand reading. He started discussing the British Royal family, referring to King George V (then Duke of York) and remarking that King Edward VII was a born diplomat. He next insisted on feeding his guest, and introduced himself as the chef who was to demonstrate his method of preparing his favorite dish, Irish stew.

Tired of elaborate meals, he had had a small kitchen fitted up in his own apartments and Cheiro was surprised to learn that the King of Belgium often cooked his own supper. As soon as the stew was ready, the King poured it into two dishes and there, at the small kitchen table, they ate what Cheiro described as "the most perfect Irish stew I have ever tasted."

Returning to the smoking room, Cheiro was urged to reveal what he saw in the King's hand, and was sternly reminded, "No flattery!" He briefly outlined the King's remarkable acquisitive and financial powers that were indicated (later substantiated by the exploitation of the Belgian Congo) and noted the King's excellent constitution. He had to point out, however, that serious trouble was likely to be expected shortly with the digestive and internal organs.

"This is your revenge for being made to eat Irish stew in a royal palace," laughed the King. "But you are wrong. I can eat anything."

Sure enough, when his death within a few years was announced, the official bulletin gave the cause as "complete breakdown of the digestive organs and intestinal obstruction."

The second reading, however, lasted fully two hours during which Leopold, though generally reckoned harsh and inflexible, behaved affably. Cheiro was impressed by the intelligence, concentration and sense of power which would have put him on top of the world had he not been a monarch. The defects of these very qualities, however, no doubt influenced his unhappy relations with his wife and family. He was greatly comforted in his declining years by his association with Baroness Vaughan, a short, stout and handsome lady to whom Cheiro was presented during his visit.

Cheiro's life again indirectly touched King Leopold, who also had a predilection for the fair sex, when the seer was consulted by the celebrated Gaby Deslys, who was uncertain what course to pursue, since both King Leopold and King Carlos of Portugal were eagerly vying for her favors.

It was during this period that Cheiro fell heir to a renowned and profitable champagne business. The vineyards in the Rheims area and bodega in Paris came to him unexpectedly in settlement of a debt he had long ago given up as a bad debt. He had the satisfaction of seeing his own "Royal Imperial" vintages served exclusively at some of the most fashionable Paris night haunts, and even got bored at having magnums of his own champagne frequently flourished at him by smiling waiters eager to turn a compliment.

Ultimately he lost this flourishing business because of the devastation wrought by the Germans in the First World War. As is well known, the Rheims district suffered severely from repeated bombardments. It became a land saturated with warfare and carnage — horribly shattered by explosives. When finally it was possible to assess the damage to his property, more than a million bottles of champagne that had been mellowing in the cool vaults were looted. The carefully tended soil was impregnated with so much antagonistic chemical matter that it was no longer able to produce the sunny fruit that had been distilled into such quantities of exhilarating nectar. The vineyards were utterly destroyed.

Not a centime's reparation came from any source for this tremendous loss, and by the time he realized the extent, he had already begun to regard, as *Fatalistic*, the financial blows received by Count Louis Hamon. No matter what opportunities for security and riches, Cheiro the Seer – his alter ego – would be instrumental in thrusting upon him, they never worked out.

Since his friendly reception by King Edward VII, on reading his hands in London when he was Prince of Wales, and in spite of accurately foretelling his death at the age of sixty-nine, Cheiro had followed his career with admiring interest. To some extent they shared the same tastes and inclinations, so each was in sympathy with the other's point of view.

Anxious to foster international friendship, Cheiro had already influenced the attitude of Nicholas II, Czar of Russia, on the subject of the Hague Peace Conference of 1899 and the famous Peace Prescript. Now he acquired the *American Register and Anglo-Colonial World*, a newspaper founded during the last days of the Empire and reputed to be the oldest English language journal published on the Continent. In its columns, which were circulated throughout well-informed French circles, he did his utmost to further a rapprochement between Great Britain and France - relations being strained at the time due to the Fashoda affair.

Knowing King Edward's deep liking for France, Cheiro wondered how a visit by His Highness would be received, and if it would help diminish the differences between the two countries. He therefore caused thousands of letters to be sent to all parts of France asking this question and was overwhelmed with replies, some long and argumentative, some abusive; but the majority evincing warm feelings towards the King personally but with guarded hostility and suspicion towards "perfidious Albion".

The British Ambassador considered the time inopportune to present such a suggestion to His Majesty, but as the French Minister for Foreign Affairs congratulated Cheiro on his newspaper campaign and applauded the idea of a Royal visit, so Cheiro himself then forwarded most of the replies to the King and recalled to him how they had chanced to meet.

A month passed during which he heard nothing from England, although his newspaper continued to print selected replies and published articles recommending an "*entente cordiale*". Then one day he was asked to call at the British Embassy, handed the letters that had been sent to the King, thanked for his trouble, and informed that arrangements were being made for His Majesty to visit Paris.

It was a most diplomatic gesture and fortunately passed off without incident, although President Loubet and others in authority were apprehensive, and every precaution for the King's safety was taken by Mons. Lepine and the French police.

Encouraged by his success, Cheiro followed this by launching another newspaper he called *Entente Cordiale*, a journal in the interest of international peace, with offices in Paris and London. He hired journalists in the principal European capitals and several responsible editors, himself scurrying with his accustomed penchant for travelling, between Paris and London, supervising final arrangements. This peaceful journal had a rather stormy birth, its international personnel falling out amongst themselves on the eve of the first issue. Fortunately a little bloodletting ventilated their grievances and they pulled together with a will to produce a very satisfactory little paper.

In the first issue, the King was given a title by which he is still referred, "Edward the Peacemaker." Within months the paper was selling all over the world. Congratulations poured in from the Four Corners, even from the Japanese Mikado. But its excellent style and presentation made it too expensive to produce, and by the end of the first year Cheiro was glad to stop his experiment in the interest of peace, at the cost of a heavy personal loss. Cheiro declared it was, in fact, the most financially disastrous enterprise he ever undertook.

On one of his many journeys across Europe, Cheiro passed through Berlin and renewed his acquaintance with the German seer, Herr Zunklehorn, known as *The Immortal*.

They first met in Cheiro's London rooms where his secretary was reluctant to admit, on a late afternoon, a frail, shabby old foreigner. But he drifted in — like some withered leaf blown by the wind — and stole Cheiro's attention as a "disciple of Althus". This was the great Greek seer who devoted his whole life to the study of the influence of gems on human beings. At the mention of the name, Cheiro's weariness vanished, though he hardly thought the battered-looking old man before him could be the custodian of similar occult secrets. Yet experience had taught Cheiro that wisdom often came from the most unlikely mouths. He regarded his visitor with fresh interest.

As the old man sank into a chair, Cheiro could see he was frail with extreme age: his bald, high skull, piercing blue eyes, curved thin nose and well-shaped mouth reminded Cheiro of portraits of Queen Elizabeth's favorite English astrologer and occultist, Dr. John Dee. Introducing himself in his peculiarly soft voice, he said he realized that his time was nearly up, and that he felt a strong need to pass on to a young and worthy successor certain information of the highest importance, - "not only in the art we both cherish, but also for the countries we represent."

He explained how he had lost favor at the German Court through forecasting to William I that his reign would not last more than twelve weeks. He was crowned with the Iron Diadem bearing a fatal gem. Zunklehorn said that if William II also insisted on wearing this ill-omened jewel in his crown, he would invite disaster. The old Seer addressed a memorandum to the young Emperor, begging him to substitute another diadem.

The Kaiser sent for him, let go a scathing attack of reproaches, and finally thundered, "I am the Kaiser! My dynasty must endure forever!!" Zunklehorn was told to withdraw — but informed that his presence at court was no longer desired.

He now begged Cheiro to come to him in Berlin as soon as possible to witness an experiment he had long contemplated. Its daring shocked the younger man, but occultism and mystery were sirens he could not resist and he agreed to go. Herr Zunklehorn was more imposing on his own ground. With his skullcap of civet fur, long robe, and his laboratory littered with old books, parchments, circles, discs, charts and strange gleaming stones, he looked the reincarnation of one of the old- time alchemists.

Like another Svengali, he produced a familiar, a young woman with a smooth, expressionless face, who was apparently in a hypnotic trance. With her as medium, he claimed to be able to "raise up the spirits of the dead, even as Samuel was brought up by the Witch of Endor."

With some ritual of mystic circles, numbers and incantations, the girl was put into a full trance. Presently a greenish pillar of light began to appear in the darkened room. It gradually assumed human, indeed superhuman semblance and through the lips of the writhing medium, issued a deep, authoritative voice: "I am Frederick the Great, King of Prussia and Margrave of Brandenburgh...."

A long interrogation followed, conducted in almost archaic German, the gist of it later being translated by Zunklehorn for Cheiro. A solemn warning was again repeated that the Kaiser was rushing toward disaster. War would come in August 1914, and he would be overthrown in 1918 - his dynasty ended and himself in exile.

The apparition faded, the medium resumed her passive calm, and glided silently out of the room. Zunklehorn expressed his satisfaction at having at last been able to summon this Great Spirit, and in Cheiro's presence.

"I leave these predictions in your hands," he said finally.

What use Cheiro may have made of them is not known. His prophecies certainly came true and no one knows whether William II made any effort, if he again had been apprised of them, to avert the causes or avoid the disaster.

So often have warnings been received and ignored by subjects, insulated by egotism and stubbornness, that one wonders how much actually can be avoided, even if peril is known beforehand. So how much is *Destiny* - a star in its fixed orbit spinning its appointed, inevitable course, a thread having its unique, unalterable place in life's tapestry - under the influence of free will to change that course, that pattern, for good or evil?

Cheiro used to say that *Destiny* is like a vessel bound for a certain, though unknown destination...The very words have affinity. Mankind, the passenger, cannot alter that course, but free will consists in the liberty to roam through the ship and use one's life span according to your "notions," inherited and acquired. Your skills may be applied to instruct, amuse or offend fellow passengers. Rewards and punishments may be unevenly distributed, but some evils can be avoided by knowing the time of danger beforehand. He also favored much more attention being paid to the signs and planets of the Zodiac and their influences on the birth date. Cheiro once even sketched out a "cult" which he felt should develop these ideas as its main tenet and which would, he thought, produce much more harmony in human relations all over the world.

Zunklehorn died in Berlin during the First World War, about 1917, but before he did, he visited Russia and was granted an audience by the Czar who never lost an opportunity to converse with a mystic. Rasputin had by that time gained in ascendancy, however, and secured the German's banishment on the pretext that he was an enemy spy.

Chapter Nine

Czars, Bandits and Chinese Mystics

It was through King Edward that Cheiro met Czar Nicholas II. Some years before, there had been a long tête-à-tête session at Marlborough House when the then Prince of Wales asked him to do the horoscopes of certain unnamed people, giving him their dates of birth. Afterwards he realized that most of these people were crowned heads of Europe. About a year later, a gentleman called at his rooms in London, showed him the sheet of paper covered with astrological notations that Cheiro had left with the Prince, and asked his reasons for making such a dramatic prophecy!

Cheiro read again his own words: "This person will be hounded all his life by the horrors of war and bloodshed; he will do his utmost to prevent them, but his *Destiny* is so closely associated with such things that his name will be bound up with some of the most far-reaching and bloodiest wars in history, and in the end, about 1917, he will lose all he loves most, by sword and strife, in one form or another, and he himself will meet a violent death."

The visitor took copious notes of Cheiro's explanations, paid him the usual fee, and withdrew without disclosing his identity. It was not until a few weeks later that a Russian lady called and told him that the Czar had recently visited him and was deeply upset by his predictions.

When he was in Russia in 1904, Cheiro was taken by Mons. Isvolsky, a Russian Minister whose exile and poverty after 1917 he also foretold, to the Czar's summer palace at Peterhof. He was impressed by the noble palace, terraced gardens, the famous golden waterfall where limpid water flowed over steps of beaten gold —but he was horrified to see the imperial yacht kept in constant readiness — full steam up — should the Czar need to flee the country — and to learn that the car in which he was being conveyed was bomb and bullet proof! The rumblings of dissatisfaction were heard even unto the throne, and these precautions belied the fatherly affection in which he was supposedly held.

To his surprise, Cheiro was taken to dine at the Palace at the invitation of the Czar and was warned, should the Czarina be present, to avoid all mention of the occult. He was welcomed by his host, who acknowledged that he visited Cheiro in London, but when the Czarina joined them for a quiet dinner, she seemed distraught and spoke little.

As they entered, the Czar looked like an English country gentleman. He was reading the London Times in his library. In deference to his guests, clad in day clothes, the Czar didn't dress for dinner. There was little or no ceremony and conversation was in English and French. Obedient to the Czar's wishes, Isvolsky also withdrew after dinner, when the Czarina left, and in the royal study Cheiro saw again the fatal paper on which he had inscribed the Czar's terrible *Destiny*. From his own lips he heard that it had been passed on to Czar Nicholas by King Edward who then confirmed it by an incognito visit to the seer.

Further confirmation had been given in the prophecy regarding the Czar's friend, Isvolsky. Now the Czar begged Cheiro to work out two horoscopes. They were those of his wife and son. Each showed a tragic *Fate*, again pointing to 1917 as the year of *Destiny*, leading to the end.

Cheiro was amazed at the calmness with which the Czar met these revelations. He made Cheiro promise not to reveal the details of what passed between them that evening, and said: "It has given me the deepest pleasure to have this conversation with you. I admire the way you stand by your conclusions."

The Czar of all the Russias rose, and they went out to join Isvolsky on the terrace, who was looking down on the imperial yacht, a seeming toy in the summer sea, yet trim and seaworthy for instant flight should the all-powerful monarch be threatened. And yet, when the time came, he did not go.

Already there were many signs that his precautions were not in vain. One morning, in his hotel on the Nevsky Prospect, Cheiro was awakened by a police officer warning him that "everyone is ordered not to look out between nine and twelve from the windows on this avenue because the Czar will pass this way to dedicate a church built on the spot where his predecessor was assassinated."

Cheiro disobeyed and cautiously peered through a slat at one window as the procession drew near. The Czar's carriage, surrounded by the Imperial Guard, dashed swiftly by, and the troops lining the Nevsky were shoulder to shoulder, not facing the royal carriage but pointing their rifles at the windows along the route, ready to fire at any sign of disturbance.

With the first snows of winter making the streets almost impassable, Cheiro saw a band of prisoners, some fifty men and a few women, handcuffed together. They had obviously been arrested while at work. Some were in shirtsleeves, some in overalls and now, numb with misery and frozen with the cold of eighteen degrees below zero, they were being driven to the station to head for the dreaded Siberia. Silence fell on the passers-by. Cheiro's driver, like many another, bared his head and made the sign of the cross. Involuntarily, Cheiro did the same.

This was Holy Russia, and this was the environment of the so-called beloved "Little Father" of his people, within a decade of the Revolution. Yet for much of the time, it was easy to ignore and to forget the menace of the future. One could drive along miles through the snowy night to some isolated mansion where lavish splendor reigned, where there were lights, warmth, music, laughter, sparkling eyes and, sparkling wines. Court life in Russia was brilliant and filled with gaiety, an eternal round of balls, parties and princely entertainment.

Backed by royal favor, smiled upon by Court circles, influenced, no doubt, by the memory of his beautiful aunt who had been a lady-in-waiting to a former Empress, Cheiro was soon an interested observer of this complicated web of intrigue that beset the Russian scene. It was a land of violence — violent climate, violent contrasts, and violent emotions. But surely it could not be the end of a regime! Blind to the logical outcome of his own prophecies, Cheiro, when invited by the Czar to invest his savings in Russian rails, placed his money in the hands of the Czar. Each time the wheels of a Russian train revolved, he stood to make money. There were many wheels and much territory to traverse. Infinite riches again beckoned. But all that went with the Revolution. With the overthrow of the Czar came another stunning reversal in the fortunes of Count Louis Hamon.

However, for the moment, all was golden. The Czar also promised Cheiro an interest in obtaining transport concessions over undeveloped lands. The offer initially materialized, and within a year or so Cheiro was back to start yet another enterprise that was doomed to fail.

While in Russia, Cheiro met the Mad Monk Rasputin through Helidor, a cultured, gentle mystic, who brought the uncouth savage, in his monkish garb, to see him. Protesting all the time, with his customary boorish arrogance, Rasputin spurned the future indicated to him in 1908.

"I foresee for you a violent end within a palace. You will be menaced by poison, by knife and by bullet. Finally, I see the icy waters of the Neva closing above you."

"Who are you who thinks he can predict the end of Rasputin?!" the mad monk raged. "Rasputin can never die! Not knife, nor bullet, nor poison can harm me. I am the savior of my people. I am greater than the Czar."

With this, to Cheiro's relief, he strode out of the room.

Rasputin's influence with the Russian royal family dated from his successfully exerting his hypnotic power over the ailing little Czarevich, their son, until he gradually, imperceptibly, abused the confidence extended to him, especially by the Czarina. Her credulous obstinate nature was filled with vague devotional meanderings.

Rasputin's introduction at Court was arranged by Mme. Gutjan Sund, whom Cheiro also met. She was a Swede married to a German officer, later prominent in the espionage service of his country. Mme. Sund had also impressed the Czar and Czarina by her occult gifts. They consulted her daily, and as a result, she was hated by the Grand Dukes. On making Rasputin's acquaintance, who at that time was building a reputation exploiting wealthy women he could persuade to be disciples of his new creed, "Sin for Salvation", Mme. Sund was quickly dominated by him.

He caused her to inform the Czarina that she had been mistaken in prophesying that the Czarevich would not live to reign, and that she now had met a saintly *Father* who could work miracles and could save the little boy's life.

The Empress sent for Rasputin. He came, arrogant, dirty and impressive, striding into her presence and crying in his bell-like voice, "Repent, ye who wear purple; repent, ye who are clothed in garments of gold and silver."

The Empress was so impressed that she fell upon her knees, and the Court entourage witnessed the amazing spectacle of the consort of the Emperor of Russia kneeling before a dirty peasant.

Rasputin told her positively that he, alone, could restore her son to health. After that, the Imperial pair were as clay in the hands of the so-called Monk. When the Imperial child fell ill shortly afterwards and was apparently at the point of death,

Rasputin dismissed all the physicians and announced: "faith alone will prevail."

One of the doctors described the scene: "I was in attendance with other Court physicians grouped around the bed of the heir to the throne, who was gasping for breath. Suddenly Rasputin strode in, made no sign that he saw the Czarina, and shouted:

'Away, unbelievers! Away! This is the work of faith!'

The startled physicians drew back as the Empress came forward, and kneeling before Rasputin, she cried:

'My Father -- save my child!'

'Turn out these dogs,' cried the Monk, sweeping his fiery glance across their outraged faces.

'At a look from the Empress,' continued the physician, 'nearly all the doctors left the apartment, even Imperial etiquette hardly restraining them from shrugging their shoulders in disgust.

'Like Elisha the prophet in the Bible who raised the widow's son, Rasputin bowed his great form over the fevered little Czarevich and stretched himself in the form of a cross upon the Hope of Imperial Russia. Those present stood petrified with amazement. The Empress, her hair falling about her shoulders, knelt at the foot of the bed, her breast heaving, her maternal tears falling like rain.

'Then - the miracle happened! The physicians had said that natural sleep alone could save the child. Rasputin rose and stood before the Empress.

'Behold thy son!' he cried, his voice booming through the great apartment. There was the Czarevich, sleeping peacefully, his little hands relaxed across the magnificent coverlet, the fiery flush of fever dying to a rose-pink on his cheeks!' "

That night the news flew through the capital and spread through Russia that Rasputin was responsible for a miracle — that the heir had been dead — and that he had raised him up!

In a burst of gratitude the Czar presented Rasputin with a million rubles, while the Czarina loaded him with gifts; but even more, his influence was fixed; nothing could shake it. Once in power, he threw off Mme. Sund. She died after a short mysterious illness, and Rasputin pronounced her epitaph. "She has finished; my work has commenced."

During his third visit to Petrograd, Cheiro was invited to dinner by the Princess Golitizen, lady-in-waiting to the Czarina.

On leaving, since it was a lovely August night, he refused the offered droshky and decided to walk to his hotel. But suddenly the weather changed, rain began to fall, and he was glad, after all, to take the droshky that had followed him. A man sheltering in a nearby doorway, hearing him give his address, joined him and asked in French if he might share the vehicle as they were going to the same destination.

Cheiro agreed, but noticed that the driver was taking them at a furious pace in the wrong direction! He asked his companion to repeat the address in Russian but found that the two were in cahoots, and he was persuaded to remain quiet by the proximity of a very businesslike revolver!

Nevertheless, his companion remained courteous, and even casual, and at last, after a long drive, they turned into the courtyard of an isolated house on the outskirts of the city. He was then conducted at pistol point into a heavily shuttered room where four laboring men were filling small brass cases, obviously destined for use as ammunition. In an inner room a woman, in a complete state of despair, was seated at a table.

"Ah, Monsieur, she is broken hearted," exclaimed his guide, in a pitying tone.

Cheiro was mystified. "Can I do anything to help her?" he asked. She started up and flung herself on her knees at his feet! Her drawn, yet beautiful face was writhing with agony.

This was why she had made the other man bring him, she cried. She was a revolutionary and came from a family of rebels, all of whom, including her husband, had paid the price of discovery. But now the police, failing to find her after Bloody Sunday, had imprisoned her son in the fortress of St. Peter and St. Paul. His family record was against him and he was under sentence of death.

The irony was that as dearly as she loved her son, she had spurned his pleas to give up the revolutionary cause, declaring that she had become a leader. But her son had been born without the spirit of revenge. Now he was going to pay for her conduct. She reproached herself bitterly.

"But what can I do in all this tragedy?" Cheiro asked. "A stranger here, what good can I do?"

The Princess with whom he had dined could plead with the Czarina, came the hurried answer. "She, too, has an only son; she surely must understand what it would be like to lose him!"

The sentence was to be carried out in two days, and the mother assured Cheiro, pointing to the men silently filling bombs in the outer room, that should her son die, so also would the Czarina and her son. Full of pity, but without much hope, Cheiro promised that he would try — even that night! The half-mad mother embraced his feet. He tore himself away and, with his former companion, drove furiously back to the city. Even though it was very late, the Princess received him, listened to his story and promised to go to the Empress at the earliest hour in the morning.

It was bad news! "I have been unsuccessful. The boy is to be shot at six o'clock tomorrow. The only concession I have been able to secure is permission for you and the mother's friend to witness the execution, and take away the coffin afterwards."

She held out some undefined hope that something better might yet be arranged, but didn't give any details. At his hotel, Cheiro found his companion from the previous night waiting for him. Words were hardly necessary, but he quietly agreed to meet him at the gates of the fortress next morning at 5:30, and said he should have a hearse there waiting to carry away the body.

Cheiro spent a ghastly night. In the heavy, foreboding dawn he took leave of the boy, who gave him a gold cross he always wore, to give to his mother. Then they left him to the care of a priest. In the prison yard, the firing squad leaned nonchalantly on their rifles. The officer arrived; the men stood to attention and, at the command, loaded their arms. A bell rang. The condemned youth was marched into the yard, escorted by two jailers, preceded by a mumbling priest.

The officer said a word to the boy, who bowed his head. The order was given, rifles snapped, and the boy fell dead in the coffin at his feet. Paralyzed with horror, Cheiro saw the warders straighten out the body, screw down the coffin lid, and throw it in the hearse. Without a word, he and his companion got into a droshky and followed the hearse to that same lonely house. They placed the coffin on a bench in the centre of the room, the same bench they used to fill the bombs. His mother, wild and haggard, watched them unscrew the lid. As the men respectfully stood back, the woman softly took her son's head to her bosom. She was so quiet and gentle...silent tears rolled down the cheeks of the men present.

Cheiro turned away, feelings he could bear no more, when all at once there was a violent scream! He rushed forward to see the boy's eyes open! He was speaking to his mother! The miracle was explained: The Princess had influenced the officer in charge of the firing squad to issue the soldiers with blank cartridges. He had instructed the boy to fall forward, as though dead, when the shots were fired. And he had involuntarily made it more realistic by fainting at that very moment!

Cheiro had good cause, for many long years, to remember the mother's gratitude. His heart was full. He went away and left them to their happiness, little dreaming that three years later, that same boy would save his life! He had gone to southern Russia, pausing at Kiev where the Zemstvo had offered him a concession to replace the antiquated public system by a service of auto-omnibuses. Unfortunately, he found that a German firm was already in negotiation over the same deal and had made a ridiculously low tender. Therefore he thought it best to withdraw. Actually, the German motors proved too light for the Kiev district, and within two years travelers were glad to return to the old-fashioned conveyances drawn by six or seven horses. The German company had failed — miserably.

He already admired Kiev's commanding position on the crest of a hill overlooking the Steppes and the Dnieper and been awed by the Grand Llarva, or Great Cathedral, its catacombs carved out of solid rock, filled with relics and treasures. The holiest relic of all, a small painting on human skin of the Madonna's head, he had been privileged to kiss, a rarely accorded honor. The picture had a long and adventurous history, bound up with that of the sacred building that housed it, and had been miraculously restored when the monks returned, after the countryside and the cathedral had been sacked by the Saracens. Since then it has been a religious custom for rich and well-meaning persons, within a great radius, to leave to the picture, at their death, one fine diamond. Consequently the gold frame, many times enlarged, was encrusted with thousands of sparkling diamonds, and picture and frame were regarded with special veneration by the devout.

Cheiro then made his way across the Caspian, glimpsed Turkestan and Mount Ararat where he was shown a piece of Noah's Ark, then retraced his steps to Tiflis, capital of the

Caucasus. Here again he was well sponsored and armed with a signed Government concession to place motor omnibuses for mail and passengers on the famous military route of Georgia, serving Vadikaffouas and Tiflis. He was told the concession was worth a fortune.

That insatiable curiosity of his led him to want to cross the Ural Mountains to see the perpetually snow-capped Kaspeck, loftier than Mont Blanc. He said his reason was a practical one -- a desire to inspect the famous route of Georgia for himself. He was the guest of the Viceroy of Georgia, Count Vorontroff-Daskoff, when he expressed this wish and was surprised when he saw the Count's look of incredulity!

"If I gave you an escort of my best Cossacks, I doubt if you would even get half-way," he laughed. "It is true, it is our great military road from north to south, constructed by Peter the Great, but since it is now so infested with bandits it would take as long as the Japanese War to clear them out, and it would cost as much in lives and money."

It was a questionable omen for the success of any peaceful bus service in the region, but a peasant caravan occasionally made the journey, and Cheiro resolved to follow his first inclination and explore the route. A Georgian Prince, looking magnificent in the uniform of a Cossack officer and armed to the teeth, for a mere bauble of consideration agreed to accompany him. As a Georgian, he said he laughed at danger and, besides, his own brother was chief of the bandits — who were, apparently, the principal scourge — so they need have no fear.

They set off in a carriage drawn by four splendid Cossack horses and were well supplied with winter clothing, furs and provisions as a precaution against the snowy, isolated country they were to travel. Cheiro bought a new Browning revolver, but even that failed to give him courage when they reached the eerie edge of the ice where the forest ceased to grow, birds ceased to sing, and *Nature* herself seemed to withdraw before this dominion of cold and loneliness. As for that Cossack, he was utterly deflated.

Their sophisticated provisions, too, looked out of place, but food they must all have, and they thought a glass of the French champagne they had brought might infuse into them fresh life and at least a semblance of bravado. But just as they had their feast spread out on a slab of massive granite, fancying themselves entirely alone, as they had seen no sign of man nor beast for hours, two huge hands appeared from behind their shoulders, took the glasses from their fingers and, with a laugh, emptied them down two fierce, capacious throats.

They were surrounded by bandits, captured, with not a word said, not a shot fired. In vain the Georgian Prince ranted — in every language and dialect he knew — in vain he threatened them with his bandit brother. Nothing. Nada. Not even a response. The bandits ate the juicy provisions, drank the champagne and left their captives two hunks of dry bread.

Away went their horses, while they were pushed into the centre of the cavalcade and marched for about an hour across the side of the mountain to their captors' fortress, a natural stronghold of rocks on the edge of a precipice, surrounded on the other side by impassable ice.

Here the bandits had made themselves pretty comfortable. In a large, log hut blazed a welcome fire and the tired captives were glad enough to relax on the rough benches surrounding it, and accept the tea dispensed by a deaf-and-mute youth who was left to guard them while the others departed on some mysterious mission. Cheiro's Georgian friend said he overheard them say they intended to hold the foreigner for ransom, the amount to be determined the following day when their chief returned from some expedition. The chief had apparently come from the north and quickly assumed command of the bandits in the two years he had been with them, and he had enormous influence with the revolutionaries of St. Petersburg.

"But the Viceroy," protested Cheiro. "Surely if I send word to him he will send the ransom to save us."

"You don't seem to realize where you are," his friend wryly smiled. "No message would ever reach him, and anyway, it would take years to find us in these wastes."

"But they don't seem to watch us too closely," the other prisoner observed. "Maybe we can escape."

They went out and looked around. There was no one to be seen and they could wander where they liked. So they climbed up on the rocks. On two sides was a precipice of unbroken rock falling sheer into an abyss, on the other side a plain of ice and snow leading to the great glaciers that rose to the peaks of the Kaspeck. The wide cleft in the black rock by which they had entered and the winding path that approached it was easily guarded by one man with a rifle.

"But our drivers! They were allowed to escape! They will give the alarm when they reach Tifilis!"

"They value their own skins too much. They have to live there, and besides, you paid them in advance. And, no doubt, the "good" Caucasians are as likely as not on the side of the bandits."

Depressed, they returned to the hut, grew hungry, and like dogs watched the deaf-and-mute youth stirring the pot of venison stew which made their mouths water. At last the bandits returned, in good humor by reason of a Robin Hood haul, and let the captives share the stew and wash it down with glasses of vodka.

But no, they still couldn't escape. Morning came and the bandits awoke. They enjoyed their tea as much as others do in more civilized environments. Then they gathered up the stolen gold which had been left carelessly lying about — mute evidence that it could neither be spent nor stolen here — and even offered Cheiro the residue of the cigarettes they stole from a passing merchant.

Then, to his amazement, the bandits washed and smartened themselves up, loaded their cartridge belts, cleaned their rifles, and went off to meet their chief. In about an hour they returned, preceded by a tall, slight figure. There was a lot of chatter in Georgian, his companion rose and gave a military salute, and even Cheiro rose to face his host since a tribute of some kind seemed to be expected.

He noticed the contrast between the appearance and physique of followers and leader. Where had he seen those steel gray-blue eyes before? ... Suddenly their owner leapt forward and clasped him in both arms — crying in French, "My God! To imagine we should meet like this!"

For a second Cheiro did not recognize him but then the most wonderful thing happened: It was those same eyes he had seen facing rifles in a prison yard in Petrograd. This was the man whose life he had saved three years before!

What a strange story he related: His mother, in the end, had been killed by the police and this had sprung to life that spirit of revenge that she could never before arouse in him. He became an outlaw and used all the money he gained to help the revolutionaries in the north.

"All men are bandits," he said bitterly, "until they become successful, and then if they have enough luck to rob countries, they become kings."

A few hours later they were on their way back to Tiflis. The bandit chief accompanied them to the very out-skirts of the town, embracing him as a brother before he bade him a final farewell...Cheiro received an offer to share the spoils and become a Caucasian bandit but declined. As regards to running a transport business in that God-forsaken place, Cheiro decided from this experience that it would be, at best, risky.

That mild obsession over, the next territory *Fate* assigned him was China and Japan. While in London he had met Marquis (later Prince) Uorubumi Ito, one of the representatives of Japan's noble families who had staked his life on the need for his country to progress along Western lines. He had shipped on as a seaman in order to leave Japan unobserved and personally evaluate the impact of Western ideas. The ideas he put forward were at first strongly opposed by Japan's conservative elder statesmen, but later adopted with a fervor and exaggeration that wrote another terrible page in world warfare. Shortly after becoming acquainted with Cheiro, the Marquis became Japanese Foreign and War Minister and urged him to visit Tokyo.

That opportunity arose sooner than Cheiro expected. During and after the Boxer Rebellion China was in a troubled state with Japan and Russia -- contending for part of its territory and the Western Powers seeking to preserve and develop their trade interests. Cheiro was requested to act as emissary for a prominent financier in some concession negotiations, and invited to be correspondent for a well-known London newspaper during his visit.

While in Tokyo, he called on the Marquis and was courteously received, but found that in his capacity of War Minister he was immersed in the strategy and tactics of the China-Japanese dispute. He then went on to Port Arthur in China where negotiations with certain War Lords were to take place. On his arrival he found everything in confusion. The Japanese were about to march a large body of troops through Manchuria, aiming to take Port Arthur. Marquis Ito went with them.

Cheiro's business made slow progress, especially in these circumstances, though Chinese methods would at any time have made it leisurely. Goodwill money had to be liberally distributed, so much, indeed, that Cheiro sent urgent messages to London asking for fresh instructions. While waiting, he used his free time to explore more of the local region. He covered hundreds of miles by means of pony relays and on one occasion was particularly struck by a magnificent dwelling set in terraced gardens on a mountainside above the main road leading from the north to Port Arthur.

As he paused to admire this enchanted palace, a train of Chinese servants, liveried in brilliantly colored tunics and embroidered with gold dragons, emerged from the gates bearing on their shoulders, slung by bamboo poles, a richly lacquered palanquin. To his surprise, the head man approached and humbly indicated that the grandee within the palanquin desired to speak to him.

The Chinese nobleman, in all the glory of his ceremonial costume, addressed Cheiro in English, told him his reputation had preceded him and that his arrival was expected. He begged Cheiro to please accept what poor hospitality he was able to provide. Thus was Cheiro introduced into the gravely charming ritual of a rich Chinese household. He was honored by being invited to use the Mandarin's own private swimming bath, a luxurious highly glazed and ornamented tank but he was perturbed by a peculiar flashing of some lustrous, jewel-like objects deep-set within a row of indentations that might almost have been holes. They were peepholes, in fact. For when he explored one with an inquiring finger, the "jewel" was withdrawn with a howl! A feminine howl. The peepholes were provided for the ladies of the household so that they might see their lord and master, or his privileged guests, at their ablutions, without themselves being seen. Cheiro took no more baths during his stay.

The first evening was spent in banqueting and conversation, the current war and the occult being the principal subjects discussed. After a night that began peacefully, the most dismal howling suddenly awakened Cheiro! It proved to come from the throats of a score of the Mandarin's wives who raged around him, apparently in agony and despair, while he sat acquiescently but seemingly unmoved, under the cherry tree in the central courtyard.

The cause of all this noise Cheiro learned, was the arrival at dawn of a Chinese runner with the news that the coming of the Japanese army was imminent! It was in full march and bearing down on Port Arthur and would pass through the road that bounded the Mandarin's estate. Judging the enemy by his own country's soldiers, he expected his house, gardens and farms to be looted and despoiled. Worse still, the shrines of his ancestors would be desecrated. He was in full agreement, therefore, with the lamentations of his wives. They expressed his own sentiments, but out of consideration for his guest he dismissed his wives to their quarters and prepared to offer prayers to Buddha.

Cheiro had an inspiration. Calling for writing materials and a swift messenger, he quickly penned a few lines to Marquis Ito who he knew would be with the Japanese army and asked him to repay the hospitality he had received from the Mandarin, by sparing his possessions. This was sent off to Japanese headquarters and the messenger was cautioned to give it only to the War Minister himself.

At sundown, after a long day of waiting, the tired messenger returned, bearing an assurance from the Marquis that orders would be issued enforcing no looting while the troops passed the Mandarin's estates. All through that night and the next day the Japanese army marched by, but the Marquis kept his word and there was no disturbance and more importantly, no looting. He and his staff brought up the rear of this great cavalcade, drawing rein for a short conversation with Cheiro before dashing onwards to Port Arthur.

The Mandarin's gratitude was only equaled by his amazement that his guest should have such influence and be able to use it on his behalf. He could think of no adequate gift he could bestow in recompense, except permission to witness some Chinese occult mysteries that were jealously guarded from the eyes of the uninitiated, especially those of foreign devils.

They were conveyed in palanquins about eight miles to a small Buddhist temple. There they removed their shoes and put on blue mantles covered with the Chinese version of the signs of the Zodiac. The Mandarin and his servants prostrated themselves before the little shrine that contained a golden statue of Buddha. A heavy trap-door in front of the shrine was lifted, and they descended a rough stone stairway into crypts and passages, eventually emerging into a subterranean grotto with a strange hole bored through the shoulder of the mountain, affording the spectator within the cave a bird's eye view into the valley, far below.

To them, from the depths of the grotto, after the priests had departed, leaving them alone, came *Ta-Theo-Tam, the Timeless and Ageless Mystic of the Mountains*. He was a repellent figure, incredibly old with glazed eyes, and had a huge spotted toad seated on his black robed shoulder. In response to a request from the Mandarin, he drew around himself on the earthen floor with his long fingernail, a circle, within which also squatted the toad, its brilliant eyes gleaming.

The ancient foretold that the foreign devil, whom he recognized as knowing something of the greater mysteries, would fail in the business now at hand. He then proceeded to show the power he possessed. A piece of smooth and shining copper was thrust into Cheiro's hands and gradually pictures emerged on it, scenes of his past life. In it he saw Marquis Ito consulting him again in his London rooms, then recognized him again in a grotesque unfamiliar city. He was in a carriage surrounded by galloping horses, his drooping body and bloodstained head supported by two men.

"Yes," said the Mandarin, as the grotto filled with cackling, devilish laughter. "Ta-Theo-Tam says war-maker devil Ito shall die by hand of Korean brother. He says gods very pleased."

Cheiro saw in the copper's reflection, the Chinese mystic shuffling into a frenzied dance, accompanied by the hopping toad. The walls seemed to recede, gloom thickened, and a stifling sensation oppressed him. The decrepit Chinese oracle was standing, larger than life, on a carved pillar surrounded by other wildly dancing figures. A great gong clanged maddeningly and a swelling incantatory chant filled the Western spectator with unnamable fears. At last the tension ebbed, the scene faded, and a fresh current of air played over the reviving man. The Mandarin bent over him, holding a cup of water to his lips, and urged Cheiro to return home with him and "let the dark visions of the cave be forgotten."

True to the vision, Prince Ito was assassinated at Harbin by a Korean assailant, member of the *Ha-Ha-Wei Tong* secret society, which had sworn death to all Japanese responsible for the victory over China. He had triumphed in strengthening his country by an alliance with Great Britain, but paid with his life for the gain of Port Arthur. A piece of it had to be conceded to Russia before they were able to wrest it away once more, establishing Japanese control in Manchuria and Korea.

Nor was the other prophecy made by the *Ageless One* less true in its fulfillment. Owing to the disturbed state of the country, and the uncertainty of those granting concessions having power to implement them, Cheiro was forced to abandon negotiations and left China with his mission unaccomplished.

Cheiro (Count Louis Hamon) at age 46

Countess Mena Hamon at age 34

Cheiro's Los Angeles Home at 7417 Hollywood Boulevard

Cheiro in his 69th year

Cheiro's signature

Cheiro's Casket with Masonic Symbol in flowers

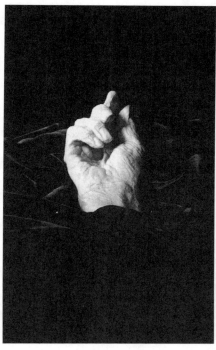

Cast of his right hand

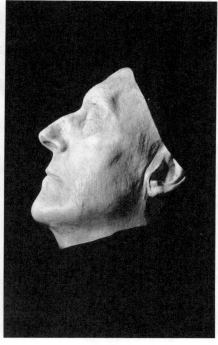

Death Mask

Famed Hollywood Mystic Passes

CHEIRO, ADVISER OF KINGS, DIES

Lives of World's Great Swayed By Seer

By GILMORE MILLEN

A man who saw destiny for kings and motion picture stars in the lines of their palms and in the number of letters in their names and so directed powerful careers in the world for years, died in Hollywood today.

He was Cheiro, his true name was Count Louis Hamon, and when death came to him, after four months of failing health, through the trees of his wooded estate at 7417 Hollywood boulevard, he was 70 years of age.

From the nineties he was the world's greatest palmist. He read lines in the hands of the Czar of Russia, King Leopold of Belgium, Mata Hara, and foretold the doom of Lord Kitchener in the sea off Scotland during the World war.

NOTED FOR PROPHECIES

He wrote a book in which he prophesied the fates of nations. By the mathematical calculations involved in the occult science of numerology he won world-wide recognition for his forecasts of coming events.

In his autobiography he told how he predicted by fadic numbers the date of the death at 69 of King Edward VII of England, when the future ruler was Prince of Wales.

Among the mighty who consulted him were also Sarah Bernhardt, Lily Langtry, Elenora Duse, Gladstone and King Humbert of Italy, Melba, Nordica Calve, Mark Twain, Ella Wheeler Wilcox, Gaby Deslys.

He claimed to have been instrumental in helping King Edward form the entente cordiale between England and France and once he worked his system of numbers at the bank at Monte Carlo, and figured out the astrological significance of the game of roulette.

TRACES ANCESTRY

His ancestry, he said, dated back to a pagan ancestor of Rollo, first Duke of Normandy. This ancestor, Hamon the Sea King, struck off with one blow of a battle ax the

Death today took Cheiro, world famous numerologist and adviser to European royalty and Hollywood stars, at his secluded Hollywood estate. Cheiro, whose real name was Count Louis Hamon, is shown above with his wife, Countess Mena Hamon, who was at his bedside when he succumbed. Cheiro was 70 years of age.

head of St. Hellier, who was attempting to convert his sailors in 526 A. D.

Another ancestor he claimed was Robert de Hamon who invaded England with William the Conqueror and furnished 400 ships and after the conquest was named Prince of Glamorganshire and given six of the largest counties of England.

Six years ago he came to Hollywood and began writing and publishing a series of books on palmistry, the fadic system of numerology, ghost stories, world prophesies, and finally his autobiography.

LEADERS CONSULTED HIM

Leaders of the motion pictures came to consult him, to have their palms read, and to have him take their names and calculate their destinies by number. Through numerology he gave advice about all matters of existence.

On the pages of a great bound guest book among the thousands of volumes in his guest room the names of scores of great stars of the screen in the past and present were written when they came to visit.

When he died the Countess Hamon, his much younger wife, was at his bedside today.

For weeks he had been under the

(CONTINUED ON PAGE ELEVEN)

CHEIRO, NOTED L. A. MYSTIC, SUCCUMBS

(CONTINUED FROM PAGE ONE)

care of a doctor and lately had lapsed into a coma.

His last work was a discussion of zodiacal astrology combined with numerology.

His wife said today his last great prediction that was fulfilled was the death of Irving Thalberg. She said the modern occult seer by palmistry alone had arrived at a conclusion that Thalberg would die of pneumonia when he died.

By many Cheiro was regarded as the greatest mystic of modern times. To him sometimes, it was said, the mysteries of the future were plain as day.

Students and friends and associates all over the world who have become adept in his learning will continue his influence many years.

Funeral services are being arranged by Pierce Brothers' mortuary.

Press coverage of Cheiro's Funeral in October 1936

Chapter Ten

Mata Hari

Mata Hari was the most notorious female spy of World War I and probably of the twentieth century. It is said her charms were devastating, and when she set her sights on a particular man, for whatever reason, he was doomed. "I can have any man I want," she was often heard to say — and she could!

But it was long before her infamous career began when, as a young woman in Paris, the paths of Mata Hari and Cheiro crossed. The notorious womanizer met the notorious seductress at the famous Moulin Rouge where the Seer was wining, dining and wenching the night away. She was sitting alone, off to one side, looking forlorn and, no doubt, feeling dejected at having not been able to secure a position in the chorus line of the famous night club because the owner said her dance was too oriental, too exotic, for his clientele.

Cheiro, probably sensing his chance to introduce himself to this incredibly beautiful woman, introduced himself: "Pardon, Mademoiselle, but I could not help notice how unhappy you look." Once he learned her story he told her, "This place is not for someone as talented as you. They wouldn't recognize art if they tripped over it."

Smiling self-assuredly and expecting a polite if not grateful rejoinder to his comment, the young seer was flabbergasted when she exploded: "Leave me be—pig!" After running through the usual gamut of apologies, Cheiro gained her confidence by a combination of charm and telling her he was a palmist and an astrologer, which, of course, immediately caught her interest.

At that time she wasn't known as Mata Hari but as Madame McLeod, and over the years would come to be known by many pseudonyms: -- Madame Zelle, Mata Hari, Baroness von Mingen and, during the war, Madame von Hontin. Actually, at the Moulin Rouge that same evening was the great playwright, poet and wit, Oscar Wilde, who was celebrating with friends.

Cheiro first met Wilde at a party in London, thrown in his honor by Blanche Roosevelt. At that party, Wilde's pudgy little hands were thrust through a curtain, without revealing his face and Cheiro said: "These are the hands of a king, but of a king who will send himself into exile." And so, on this night at the Moulin Rouge, it was "the gay blade" who suggested to Cheiro he go over and introduce himself to Madame McLeod.

They struck up a friendship—a very, very close friendship—and for many years and in whatever city they happened to simultaneously find themselves, a burning, hot affair ensued. Cheiro often said, as did many men, "That even though she possessed a captivating beauty, her heart was as dark as her eyes, and I knew I would be lost forever should I ever submit to them. She was merciless and had no regard for any man. In my own nature, something of it requires that a woman has to have some feelings, some regard for her fellow man. She had none whatsoever. And that's what saved me."

Born Margaretha Zelle at Leeuwarden in the Netherlands on August 7 1876, Mata Hari's father was a successful hat merchant who went bankrupt and abandoned her along with her mother and three brothers when she was thirteen. Two years later her mother died and she ended up with her godfather for a year before leaving home to become a school teacher. When she was eighteen, she fell in love with a Captain Rudolph MacLeod a Dutch army officer of Scottish descent. They had two children, a boy and girl -- and moved to a military posting on a South Seas island, but the marriage soon soured because, according to her, her husband was a notorious womanizer who beat her. She grew to hate him.

Then tragedy struck on May 2, 1898, when both of her children were poisoned. Her daughter survived, but her son was dead before the doctor arrived. She suspected the gardener, who disliked her husband intensely, and assumed — rightly or wrongly — that he killed the child with poison. She returned to Holland with her daughter but eventually turned her over to her husband. Free of all ties, she turned to Paris. Free, except for the burden of anguish she was carrying.

She arrived in Paris in 1903 and debuted as an exotic dancer on March 13, 1905, in the Musee Guimet. She was an overnight success and toured Spain, Monte Carlo and Germany until 1912. Before her success, she endured hard times. It was soon after her arrival in Paris—broke! —that she met Cheiro at the Moulin Rouge. Cheiro invited her to his home where he fed and no doubt bedded her.

After that first meeting, it was quite some time before their paths crossed again. He was staying at London's palatial Dorchester Hotel, as the special guest of King Edward VII, for whom Cheiro regularly made predictions, and about whom the king always referred to as "the man who will not let me live past my sixty-ninth year." (And he didn't!) Late one night, as the Seer was examining the Monarch's hand, the telephone rang and a familiar voice came over the wire: "Cheiro, my dear friend, I need you to take a look at my chart and tell me what you see for the future."

"Why the urgency?" queried the mystic.

"The tide has suddenly turned in my favor, and I have been offered a wonderful opportunity. What is it that Shakespeare said? 'There is a tide in the affairs of men, which, if taken at the flood, leads on to greatness?' I am leaving tomorrow for Berlin, where I have been offered a lucrative position teaching dance. I will have my own suite of rooms and as much money as I need. Isn't it wonderful? I am coming to your room for a quiet hour or two. I have ordered champagne for us, as a way of celebration. Leave the door unlocked, and dismiss your valet."

She looked so beautiful in a gown of shimmering gold and sparkling jewelry that she bore little resemblance to the attractive but waif-like individual Cheiro had met in Paris. She was even more alluring, if that was possible, erudite and sophisticated. In London she was known as Baroness von Mingen and told people that German government officials were grooming her for her new teaching position. Cheiro looked at her birth chart and explained that although a very positive period in her life was about to commence, ultimately the cycle would reach its peak around October, 1917, when he told her: "*it will end for you in some kind of violent and fatal denouement.*" Cheiro warned her to get out—now—before it was too late!

She merely laughed, tossed back her head and that magnificent dark, curly mane, and replied: "Oh no, not now— just when I've got everything I want. After the terrible legacy left me by my no-good husband -- heartache, nothing but heartache. No, it shall be as you always say, Cheiro ...*c'est la vie.*"

They toasted her new career into the wee small hours, until only the glowing embers of the once roaring fire remained. When he awoke at dawn, she was gone.

History records, as far as anyone can follow the story, that she reached Ireland, at some point, was picked up by a German submarine waiting off the coast which took her to Europe, from there she could have escaped to Canada or America, since she knew police of every country were on the lookout for her.

Instead, she tempted *Fate* by returning to France and again played the role of a dancer. One night, as she slipped across "no man's land" to give vital information to the Germans, she was captured, moved to Paris and sentenced to the death of a spy.

On a cold, drizzly October morning in 1917, she kept her date with *Destiny*, right down to the day and year that Cheiro had predicted. Actress and soldier of fortune to the end, she refused the blindfold, kissed her hands to the soldiers and met her *Fate* with a smile on her lips

Legend has it she made a pact with the Captain of the firing squad, who was a former lover, to fall as though dead the instant the blanks were fired, thereby escaping once again. Some say the bullets ripped through her body and she died instantly, others say she escaped to America and lived out her years in the mid-west.

She gave her all to the people who treated her kindly, the Germans. Human *Nature.* Americans see Benedict Arnold as a traitor, but Britain and Canada see him as a hero. When her time came, she died as she had lived, bravely and with a certain *joie de vivre*.

Chapter Eleven

Slings and Arrows

Luck is a queer thing. Apart from clever management of their resources, there is little doubt some people have more of it than others, and there are periods in most people's lives when the luck is with them and their affairs prosper.

As Shakespeare observed:

There is a tide in the affairs of men which,
taken at the flood, leads on...

But, there are other times when it seems that nothing turns out, even though one person seems the same as another and his talents and efforts are applied with the same care and determination and in the same direction.

Such a period was now beginning for Count Louis Hamon. He had devoted the twenty-one years that he promised his Indian instructors in the service of hand reading. It was an exciting, exacting occupation, but at the same time stimulating and exhausting — mentally, emotionally and psychologically — and although he had been accorded respect he could not ignore the fact that his work was mocked and despised. He saw the study he esteemed used as a game, a diversion for parties and fairs — and, in dubious hands, employed to delude the credulous when indiscreet revelations had been uncovered — even used as an instrument of blackmail.

Then, too, for the few who sincerely wanted the knowledge he could impart, to conserve their spiritual assets and improve the use of their life span, there were also the many sensation-seekers desiring only another stimulus to titillate their jaded palates or guide them through the mesh of their emotional intrigues. Many times, especially at the end of an exhausting day, he yearned to get outside the strangely successful being who was Cheiro, and sink himself in the less spectacular life of Louis Hamon, gentleman and bon-vivant, a man with many enterprises — yet with enough leisure time available to enjoy the social rounds and the company of his diversity of friends.

Yet he who saw the future of so many was unable to delineate much of his own. Oh, he could tell the main events — here a shock, there a reversal, now a success — travel, sickness.... He knew he would marry fairly late in life. In the meantime, he enjoyed the attentions of many desirable women.

He indicated the likely cause of his death, and later foretold its exact day and hour. But the details of his own *Fate* and of those near to him eluded him. It was as though a veil were drawn between his second sight and those whose *Destiny* he particularly wanted to read. So much did he choose to be guided in his revelations by unconscious knowledge and intuition that he preferred to be unaware of his callers' identity — or anything about them!

Then, too, his health was beginning to disturb him. He had always been inclined to watch and pamper it, since his boyhood. Cheiro had three extra notches on his spinal column. While skating on the ice as a boy, he fell, which fractured these protruding bones. This wasn't discovered until a considerable time had passed because he didn't disclose the accident and suffered untold agonies in silence for many years as a result.

This had a permanently weakening effect on his whole system. The nervous system of most psychics and mystics is so delicately constructed and finely tuned that such individuals are often called, though less popularly, sensitives. At the end of his first London season, it was apparent that a change of scene and routine were urgently needed. During those early years in the United States, the constant travelling and changes of food and climate brought on a severe bout of pneumonia -- an illness much more serious in those pre-antibiotic days -- from which he convalesced in California and Mexico.

Reviewing his activities in the first decade of the new century, Cheiro had much cause for satisfaction but also for misgivings. He had devoted most of his time to Europe and had been on friendly terms with many notable people — conquerors and kings. He had not made nor lost a fortune in the Klondike Gold Rush, nor through his Chinese concessions. The Russian transport venture had proved...nearly fatal! And his journalistic experiment for peace, *Entente Cordiale,* was financially nearly fatal.

On the other hand, he had a flourishing champagne business. The *American Register and Anglo-Colonial World* continued to be profitable. His Russian rail investment was paying dividends. And people everywhere were always willing to consult him as Cheiro, the Seer.

Around this time he was brought into contact with several new activities through the association with the aristocratic widow of a German banker who seemed to have an entrée, by birth and marriage, into various exalted social circles. Unfortunately Cheiro did not learn until too late that some of them were not always desirable.

A great deal of money constantly passed between the European capitals. It was the era of private banks manipulated by the skilful few. While he was living chiefly in Paris, his new friend urged Cheiro to make use of this, as an aspect of his wide influence. She realized he had little commercial aptitude or experience and so put him in contact with a Mons. Lervé, who, as a financier and banker, could handle the detailed administration of his business venture in Paris. At first all went well with this new project, and many of his friends and clients needed little persuasion to entrust the discreet handling of some of their funds to the crony of royalty and the successful seer, who, without telling them, already knew much about their business affairs.

On his last visit to Russia he had found its barbarous extremes of climate too much for him. He was already feeling unwell when he received a telegram from his friend containing the terrible news: "following some complaints by clients, an inquiry had been ordered into the affairs of the bank and Lervé has absconded." She warned him that should he now return to Paris he would certainly be held for questioning. To avoid this, he was advised to go back to England via Holland or Belgium.

Too late he realized he had gotten in over his head and lent his name and reputation to something he did not understand, not knowing the details of the transactions to properly explain them — especially to an informed and hostile questioner. He was in agony trying to decide, made worse by physical malaise. Finally, feeling more dead than alive, he took the advice from the Baroness, crossed Europe via Brussels, reached London, collapsed with pneumonia, was removed to a nursing home and then stayed in his bed for three, long, weary months.

He bitterly repented his association with the Baroness and with the all too clever Lervé, and reproached himself that he had neither the time, the inclination nor the ability to examine Lervé's methods more closely. And he was ashamed that his friends suffered financially because of their trust in him.

Although he was reluctant to speak of this distasteful episode in later years, investigation proved it less disgraceful and disastrous than first feared. Cheiro then resolutely set himself the colossal task of paying back the losses of his friends. By now, and indeed, until the end of his life, he also had some of these pensioners on his books, often people, celebrated in their day, who had fallen on hard times. For perhaps a single casual kindness bestowed on him in their heyday, a gesture never forgotten, he considered himself their banker for years, only death itself released him from this self-imposed obligation.

Therefore when health slowly returned to him in London, though a little of the former elasticity was already gone, the money he could allocate for his personal use was nearly depleted, and he once again turned his back, with a sigh, on Count Louis Hamon and resumed his career as Cheiro with even greater intensity. His appointment book was as full as he could manage and this occupation, generally regarded as precarious at best, meant for him safety and prosperity, while the more mundane affairs that mankind engaged in without a second thought, for him always turned out tragic.

He resolved to make London his headquarters and looked around for a suitable place to live that would be more spacious and more homelike than the hotels and flats which had housed him all those wandering years. He wanted something withdrawn, an air of privacy, perhaps a touch of the rural, yet near the heart of town.

"He who seeks will find," and it seemed just the answer to his requirements when he discovered Devonshire Lodge, an old house in a discreet neighborhood set back in a large garden, whose tall trees and other vegetation sheltered it from the gaze of the passer-by. It attracted Cheiro so much that even though there were no notices up indicating it was to be let or sold, he thought he would, as usual, follow his intuition and make inquiries. Pushing open the heavy oaken door, he found himself in a peaceful, yet neglected, walled garden with a quaint fountain overgrown with moss, splashing gently as if it had been doing so forever. The house, with its low, diamond-paned windows, looked sleepy and a little gloomy. "Perhaps the place was deserted," Cheiro thought. Having come this far, he decided to pull on the heavy iron bell.

To his surprise, the door was opened by an elderly gentleman instead of the expected servant. The frail man was in the midst of explaining that the house was not available, when his wife interrupted, saying she had just made up her mind to put it in the agent's hands.

The oak-paneled lounge hall, with its beamed ceiling and open hearth, gave a warm welcome to the visitor hesitating on the threshold, and then some curtains were drawn aside revealing that the room ended in a small chapel, lit by a stained glass window. Other rooms were equally inviting and Cheiro soon decided that he would take the house if the terms were at all suitable.

"But why do you want to get rid of the place?" he asked.

There was a curiously questioning look in her eyes, as she replied: "The trouble is no servant will stay, no matter what I pay them. I won't try to deceive you. The servants' rooms are in the back, the old part. They hear noises. Queer knocks. Sometimes they think they see things. Lately, the knocks have begun in other rooms. My husband is so deaf he doesn't here them, but it has got on my nerves and I will be glad to go if I can get someone to take over the lease."

She said they had occupied the house for about a year, following the death of her husband's uncle, an eccentric who had lived there with his butler for some years, occupying only the front part of the house and leaving the older back rooms vacant and unused. After some discussion, terms were agreed upon, the new tenant stipulating that the house should be handed over to him empty at the end of two weeks.

When the time came, Cheiro was as happy as a lark. He wandered through the house, telling himself with what care it should be groomed and polished — all except one room, in the old part, leading off the stairs, below the hall. Neither he nor the decorators could determine just what to do with it and finally decided to just leave it for the time being.

He was so enthusiastic about the place that he moved in even before the decorators had finished, fitting up two rooms for his secretary and himself, hoping that the work would then be more quickly completed rather than waiting to refer decisions to his snatched daily visits.

For the present they only wanted to sleep there, getting their meals outside, so any servant problem was temporarily avoided. Carefully securing all windows and doors, they retired to their respective rooms, lulled by the surrounding stillness and the rhythmic hum of distant traffic. Cheiro read awhile, then switched off the light, happily reflecting, as he drifted off to sleep, that the refurbishing was progressing satisfactorily and that he was at last established in his own place.

In this semi-waking condition, his attention was suddenly galvanized by a noise in the house. It sounded like a door closing in the basement! His memory quickly visualized all the doors and himself in the act of fastening them. On this still night there was no wind to slam a door. He listened again. Now he heard footsteps, measured, deliberate, but not furtive.... They were on the basement stairs, leading to the hall.

He sat bolt upright, straining his ears — trying to picture the unseen intruder winding his way between the decorators' ladders. The steps came nearer, up the uncarpeted staircase, toward their rooms. He was afraid to switch on his light, reasoning that its gleam beneath the door would lead the steps directly to him. The landing near his room creaked. There was a pause. Then slowly, they continued, shuffling so close to his door that Cheiro was sure he could hear breathing! He fervently hoped the brass bolt would hold — but quickly slipped out of bed and grabbed an iron poker — putting a finger on the light switch, as though it were a gun trigger, ready to flick it on should the door burst open to reveal...as he imagined...the burglar.

Instead, he heard a loud "RAT-A-TAT-TAT!" of knuckles on the door. It dawned on him that his visitor was supernatural! A shrinking dread of the uncanny replaced his former fear. Again came the knock. Impelled by sheer terror — and without stopping to think — he switched on the light, drew back the bolt and flung open the door —!

The passageway was dark and completely empty, but before he could breath a sigh of relief, the exact knock was repeated close to his ear — on the open door! He jumped back, slammed the door, shot the bolt and spent the rest of the night sitting, shivering on his bed waiting for — he knew not what!

At last, daylight relieved his vigil. Through the window he could see the distant traffic beginning to lumber on its way. Solitary workmen passed, then tradesmen, and later a stream of city-goers. In an everyday atmosphere he began to laugh at his fears, dressed and went downstairs. With the morning sunlight and litter of ladders and painting materials, all looked reassuringly normal.

"Well, Perkins," said Cheiro as he entered the room, "did you have a good night?"

His secretary, a level-headed man, twenty years his senior, replied: "Did you?" He, too, had heard the footsteps and knocks and not for all the money in the world would he stay there another night! He urged Cheiro to give back the keys, vacate the house, and ask for a refund.

"Not so fast, Perkins," objected Cheiro, reminding him that he had been informed in the first place that servants would not stay because of the knocks and noises they heard. It was admitted that the place was haunted.

"I'm going to keep the house, whatever happens," he said. "And furthermore, Perkins, I'm going to keep you. Yes I am, my friend. You've too much good old North of England blood not to fight it out to the finish - even with a ghost!"

And fight it out they did. The next night they made a good fire in Cheiro's room, laid in a supply of sandwiches and strong, hot coffee and settled themselves in two easy chairs to await events.

By one o'clock, nothing happened. They were both dozing when the former evening's procedure began to repeat itself. A door banged, footsteps ascended, boards creaked, steps shuffled nearer — and again came the determined knocks on the door. They sprang from their chairs and stared — wide-eyed! — at one another, wordlessly. Then they heard a sharp click from the landing...someone, or something, switched on the electric light.

"Good God! That can't be a ghost," said Perkins.

They each clutched a poker and Cheiro again flung open the door. It was no longer dark but the landing was quite empty! Together they tiptoed to the top of the stairs.... No one. Nothing.... And yet the lights were on in the hall below.

"We can't leave them like that," Cheiro whispered. "We have to go down and turn them off!"

Slowly, unwillingly, pokers in hand, they crept down. An open door showed the brass light switches gleaming in the dark dining room. Was anyone lurking in there? Then, right before their eyes — click-click-click — the lights were switched on but that room was empty too! Suddenly a hollow, croaking, sneering laugh rushed past their heads, and with one GREAT leap they both turned and fled back to Cheiro's room — panting as they leaned against the closed door, its bolt safely in position once more.

Next morning when the painters came, they found the lights switched on all over the house! No explanation was vouchsafed. The new tenant and his secretary were too tired — and glad to sleep through the day, comforted rather than disturbed by the human noises of paint scraping and shifting ladders.

After a good dinner they felt more courageous.

"Well, Perkins, are we going to see it through?"

Yes, he was game for anything. He still could not believe a ghost had trodden so firmly and switched on lights, and uttered that cackling laugh! Someone must be hoaxing them to get them out of the place, for some reason! He got a dog and proposed to set it on any intruder — while he himself called in the police.

Cheiro's previous experiences indicated that dogs were even less comfortable in the presence of the supernatural than humans. Still, if it should really be a burglar.... Anyway, they were glad to have the dog as they entered the dark empty house, and it was just as delighted to see them! They gave him his supper and then he accompanied them as they all made the nightly rounds, fastening doors and windows. He sniffed and barked in every room — except that little one on the half-landing that still remained untouched. Here, he refused to follow them; his hair bristled and he whined — and trembled in every limb! They withdrew to their rooms with its lights and cozy fires. The dog was still trembling.

One o'clock ... the steps came again ... this time heavier, more distinct than before. The two men grabbed pokers; the dog sat up — alert, but silent. This time a loud "Bang!" at the door, not the familiar rat-a-tat; then a rough human voice said, "What the hell's going on in this house?" The dog began barking furiously — when all at once a strong push sent the bolt flying and a massive London policeman, in bad temper, stood at the door.

They were overjoyed to see him in spite of the impatient repetition of his question. Receiving no answer, he explained that he had found their back door closed and barred when making his first round. The second time it was unbolted and wide open — right before his very eyes! He found other doors open, every light in the place on, and the two men before him locked with a dog in one room of an empty house.

"What's the game — that's what I want to know?!" declared the officer.

They felt it was useless to venture any psychic justification in these circumstances, and so answered meekly that they had fastened up the place and could not explain the happening anymore than he. Spurning this lame reply, he insisted on searching the premises in case anyone was hiding there, and suggested they go with him. This, they were only too pleased to do, again accompanied by the dog, except for that small back room which he again refused to enter. There were no further manifestations after the policeman's departure. Once again the doors were fastened, and when daylight came they went to bed.

For a few weeks nothing more happened; then one day, when Henry Hamilton, the dramatist, dropped in to see him, he chanced to say, "I quite envy you having this old house in the heart of London. But tell me, have you had any queer experiences in it since you took it over?"

"What kind of experiences do you mean?"

"Some friends of mine lived here a few years ago and heard noises and knocks all over the place. They gave up the house because of it. I will write down and place in an envelope, a message spelled out by the knocks in this very room! Lock it up in your desk and do not open it until at some time a message is again rapped out. Then, compare the two and let me know if they are alike."

Cheiro promised, but as the days and nights went by without further incident, he forgot about the envelope. One evening, about a month after he had settled in, he asked a few friends to dinner for a little housewarming party. Afterwards, as they sat around with their coffee and cigarettes in the lounge, knocks began to sound on a crystal flower bowl that sat in front of a little figure of Buddha that was in the tiny chapel at the end of the room.

Someone suggested that the ghost should be asked to spell out his name. They sat around a table and a curious story emerged: The visitor was a Karl Clint, a German, who occupied the place as a farmhouse between 1740 and 1800. He was mixed up with the disappearance of a man named Arthur Liddel who was last seen in his company. Years later, all trace of Karl Clint was also lost. The farm became streets and the property changed hands many times. The local archives substantiated this information. But in his first message, Clint alleged that in the mysterious little back room he had murdered Liddel and buried him below the floor. He asked the modern intruders to go away and leave him in peace. The message written in the sealed envelope proved to be identical almost word for word!

As soon as Cheiro tried to make use of this room, the knockings began again — and equally promptly, some of his servants gave notice. Cheiro resolved to solve the mystery and called in the blind medium, Cecil Husk, through whom he had already had communication with his own father.

From the peculiar life that Cheiro led for so many years, and from the hundreds of confessions that men and women poured into his ears, he had lost all sense of prejudice or a desire to judge or condemn any person, no matter what crime they might have committed.

He gathered some interested friends to witness whatever would transpire, and no sooner had the séance opened, than manifestations began. It was a weary, haunted, lonely face that materialized as Karl Clint. All present could see even the texture of the skin and the reddish close-cropped hair and beard. He was approaching fifty, an intelligent looking man of peasant or farmer class.

After some preliminaries, the guttural voice repeated, "No one can help me. I only want to be left in peace."

"But you are not at peace. If you were, you would not come and frighten people as you do," answered Cheiro.

"I cannot get away. Since the night I died I am here all the time."

"You told us you murdered Liddel. Why?"

"Liddel would not leave the woman I lived with alone. I loved Charlotte more than any man ever loved a woman. He was always coming here tempting her with his money! One night he went too far. I killed him as I would a mad dog. People call such an act murder, but I would do the same thing all over again if he and I were still alive! I dug a hole in the ground under the room downstairs. I filled it with quicklime, put his body in it and what is left is still there, as far as I can tell."

"What became of Charlotte?"

"She died a few years later. She helped me get rid of the body but never got over the worry and the dread of my being found out. I buried her in the graveyard, not far from here."

"And what became of you?"

114

"After she died, I went back to Germany. I never knew a moment's happiness after Charlotte went. Life for me was torture. In the end, I committed suicide."

"And then?"

"I don't know how it came about, but all at once I seemed to wake up in the room downstairs and have been here ever since."

"But would you not like to leave this place and get away?"

"Why should I? This was the only place I called home. I was happy here with the only woman I ever loved. It was the only happiness I ever knew. Why should I leave? There is no place else for me to go."

"But Charlotte?"

"Charlotte is here, with me.... We live the old happy days over and over until Liddel comes — then I kill him again!"

"But surely there is something I can do to help you," Cheiro could not help saying.

"There is one thing," the voice replied. "Leave the room downstairs untouched. Put two chairs and a table there and allow no one to enter after dark. If you do this, you will have the rest of the place to yourself, and I will give you no more trouble."

Thus was a bargain struck with a ghost. For his part, Cheiro placed two chairs and a table that night in Karl Clint's room. And whether or not it was for this reason, nothing more was ever heard of from the ghostly resident again; no more knocks or noises. The visible world returned to its undisturbed state, the servants stayed, and Cheiro was many times envied for his unique find, an old house with an air of character, set back in a semblance of rural seclusion, yet in the heart of a teeming metropolis.

Shortly after, Cheiro contracted pneumonia and was dying. The wealthy, naïve young girl, for whom Cheiro had read so many years earlier, predicting her first husband would leave her a widow and that circumstances beyond her control would for a seven year period prevent a second marriage to a man she would meet over and over again, in every corner of the world, came to his rescue. She was now a graceful, beautiful woman. Here, in her own words, is the story of how they were finally united by *Fate*.

Chapter Twelve

Marriage

Mena found out that Cheiro was dying and hastened to his side. After her return from Egypt she settled down in England and renewed her relationship with her son, Jack[1], the only child from her disastrous first marriage. He had spent most of his early years in the care of nurses and governesses under her mother's roof. Now that he was a schoolboy, Mena had taken a house in Devon for his holidays, and it was towards the end of the summer that she chanced to read an announcement in a newspaper:

> *We regret to announce that Cheiro, the well-known seer, is so seriously ill with double pneumonia that he is not expected to live. If any relatives should see this announcement, they should come to him at Devonshire Lodge, London, without delay.*

Without a moment's hesitation, she knew what her course must be. She made arrangements for her son's care and return to school, shut up the house, and took the next train for London.

Cheiro and Mena were no longer strangers. They had met several times in various parts of the world, from China to Peru, since her first impulsive declaration in his rooms, all those years ago. She did not know whether each time he remembered it he was amused or startled, but many a time when she did, the color rose to her cheeks at the thought of her youthful temerity. And yet she had recognized instantly that this man was her *Fate*, and acknowledged it. Had she been a little older, a little more world-wise, her inhibitions and modesty might have restrained her.

Yet as much as she might blush for her impetuous utterance years earlier, she could not find it in her heart to condemn her younger self -- for she still felt the same sentiment, although now its expression was different.

But in our inner selves, how little people change! she met Cheiro many times since then, and with outward calm.

---

[1] Her son was killed in WWII; he died without children.

They were good friends and nothing more. He got on well with women but was regarded as a confirmed bachelor, having resisted the most determined feminine onslaughts, and they were many!

Yet when the appointed time came and Mena learned that Cheiro might not even exist in the same world anymore, she acted just as impulsively. By this time, of course, she had more poise and *savoir faire*, so when she arrived at his house she calmly paid for her cab, took her valise, and on being met by the nurse, announced herself as a relative who had come to take charge.

The nurse was immensely relieved. The servants were doing just as they pleased without supervision and eating their heads off! The second nurse had even failed to return! Cheiro needed constant attention, and she was worn out. He was lying in a coma, and the main nurse expected the end could not be more than a few hours away.

"I will take over," Mena said, laying aside her hat and veil. "You go off and have a good rest. Don't come back until the morning."

"But he may die before then," she stammered. "The doctor doesn't expect him to last out the night!"

"I will be responsible to the doctor," Mena replied firmly. "Do as I say. He won't die today — nor for a good many tomorrows."

The nurse really was exhausted, and after some more protestations she was glad to leave. Mena went into Cheiro's room determined not to be shocked. But she was. His old demon, pneumonia, had attacked him again and this time had laid him low, indeed. There he lay motionless, a long splendid wreck of a man, scarcely breathing, his limbs and features already composed, like those of some knight of old, on his tomb. Mena felt his head, his hands and feet. They were cold. She then rushed about filling hot water bottles, which she placed here and there. She piled on more blankets and using an old Egyptian trick, she inserted attar of roses in his nostrils and clung to his body, endeavoring to will him to live and to breathe life once more into his limp frame.

It was a long fight, but she won. When the nurse returned in the morning, bright-eyed, rested and ready to prepare Cheiro's body for burial, he was sleeping peacefully. When he awoke, he was able at last to take a little nourishment. He accepted Mena's presence naturally and gratefully, perhaps being too weak to protest and as she coaxed him back to health, Mena grew accustomed to his eyes following her around the room with a look of dependence, which they never wholly lost. He was a man who needed an inner source of strength on which to lean in his private life. Immersed as he was in the affairs and emotions of others, he returned to his own life with a slight sense of bewilderment, of being lost in the world that was real. Ironically, he was more at home in regions where others felt strange.

While he lay sick, Mena assumed the management of his household. The servants, although loyal and in their way devoted, had grown slack and extravagant with a master who was frequently both absent and absent-minded. Bills mounted alarmingly. The secretary looked after his business affairs, conferring with Mena regarding the postponement of professional engagements. When his steps at last grew stronger and he was well on the way to convalescence, she took him on a Mediterranean voyage. The warmth, the long sunny days, the peaceful motion and ever-changing scenes soon reinvigorated him and one day he came up from the writing room and handed Mena a letter and asked her to post it for him at the next port.

It was his resignation from an anti-marriage society to which he had belonged for nearly thirty years. And with this quaint prelude they were married on the way back to England. His prophecy of Mena's future had at last come true, while his own hand's indication of a marriage late in life had also been fulfilled. The year was 1913, he was forty-seven and she was ten years younger.

Mena's first husband had disappeared at sea when his ship went down with all hands eleven years earlier, and no less an authority than the eminent solicitor Marshall Hall, a personal friend of Cheiro, advised them to presume him dead and go ahead and get married.

"Why don't you two get married?" he asked. "Should Mena's first husband ever turn up, which is most unlikely, I will defend you for nothing. The publicity would be worth it."

Mena soon found, however, on their return to London that Cheiro was coveted by others. No announcement had been given of their marriage, and for the present, Cheiro returned to Devonshire Lodge and Mena to her own nearby house; he to soften the transition, in regard to his closer feminine friends, and Mena to break the news to her son.

Many women at the time thought she took a great risk. She sometimes wondered herself if she had acted rightly, but later events justified her course of action.

Cheiro was -- and it is not unknown among popular men -- a little cowardly in personal relations. He appreciated being in demand. He liked voices to lift, eyes to brighten, at his approach. He hated to offend, or give pain, and so he gently eased off the friendships that were likely to pursue him with jealousy, yet put off telling the blunt truth.

But he had grown used to Mena being around, if not actually in his presence. He then felt he could relax, undisturbed by major worries or trivial details. So he set himself to play the gallant suitor to his own wife. There were daily visits, notes, flowers and gifts. He consulted her about everything. Sometimes he would stay overnight, or for the weekend, and she was in and out of his house at all hours. He treated her as his mistress, when she was in fact, his wife! The servants at both houses thought it was scandalous, but it was just the sort of situation that Cheiro found piquant and amusing.

Mena's mother and aunt, finding Cheiro coming and going so much when they happened to call - although they, like most people, were quickly subjugated by his charm - took Mena to task.

"Don't you think you are seeing rather too much of that man? Won't people talk? Is this wise?"

"Well, seeing that I have been married to him for six months, it hardly matters if they do talk. And yes, I do think it's wise," Mena replied.

That, of course, let loose an avalanche! Why hadn't they been told - and why hadn't they been invited to the wedding? And so on. Mena began to realize the wisdom of acting first and leaving the talking until afterwards.

It was not until two years later that a party was given to meet Countess Hamon. What a barrage she faced from the women in the drawing room, after they left the men to their port and cigars! Mena had been ceremonially garbed for the occasion and had been warned not to rise to any barbs or malice, but to act the sweet ingénue. The facts of her long residence abroad in various parts of the world, and of having been presented to the King and Queen, told in her favor in this grilling social *viva voce*. To make a long story short, she was accepted. If their dear Cheiro must have a wife, they seemed to say, he might have done worse.

When they had made their smiling adieux and loaded Mena with invitations for the coming week, only then did Cheiro put his arm round her shoulders, smiled down at her and said, "I'm proud of you."

They did a great deal of entertaining during that period and gave and attended many lavish parties. They grew accustomed to being in houses where discretion was assumed as a *sine qua non,* where celebrities let their hair down, royalty casually dropped in, and where the social round covered many equally casual and confidential, international political moves.

They also acquired a comfortable old riverside home at Henley and retreated there with congenial guests for weekends, which combined luxury with the free-and-easiness of Bohemia. For Cheiro instinctively sought the best in all worlds, including people and things.

During the first part of the 1914-18 war, Mena was attached for a time to a nursing unit which saw the horrors of warfare close at hand in service at Calvados, and Cheiro was on patrol duty over a section of the Thames River in his motor launch. Later, he invented and perfected a special process of making activated carbon and artificial coal, which in its turn led to new pastures but they also shared the hopes and anxieties of London residents, with occasional respites at Henley.

Shortly before Lord Kitchener's departure on his last ill-fated journey on the *Hampshire*, Cheiro was called to Buckingham Palace. He returned with a very grave face, but as usual said nothing of what had transpired. He never told Mena the many secrets of which he was the repository. However, late one night a few days later, he instructed the servants to stay away from the front door and told them that he would personally admit the caller who was coming. He was expecting Lord Kitchener.

He had consulted Cheiro years before, first as a young officer and then when he was at the War Office in 1894, as Sirdar of the Egyptian Army. At that time Cheiro told Kitchener that he would die in his 66th year, about June, and that it either would be caused by water, probably disaster at sea, or some form of capture by an enemy and an exile from which he would never recover.

"'Thanks," he laughed, "I prefer the first proposition.'"

He even joked about his immunity from bombs and bullets, "because I know I shall die at sea," and suggested that if it should come true, he would try to send Cheiro some sign by thought transference.

But there was no laughing this night, as Cheiro led him upstairs to his study. There, they remained closeted together for a long time.

On the way out Kitchener kissed Mena's hand in what proved to be a last farewell as he left the house. His spare figure in the full-length dark military overcoat disappeared into his long, low car that drew alongside and just as unobtrusively, glided away. Cheiro went back up to his study and buried his head in his arms on his desk, and wept. Various charts were scattered about, just as Kitchener had left them.

"I feel as if I have sent a man to his doom," Cheiro said to Mena.

It is now a matter of historical fact, although perhaps little realized that the British Royal Family offered asylum in England to their cousin Czar Nicholas II and his family. And Kitchener, whose military reputation was revered in Russia, may well have had the role of royal messenger thrust upon him, in addition to his official mission.

Cheiro's prediction of possible capture and exile, which he foretold years before, may have had the Bolshevik revolutionaries in view as his captors, rather than the Germans.

Kitchener was having a difficult time with those in power in England and his formerly almost supreme power and influence were declining. And along came this questionable Royal mission, which would undoubtedly provoke more internal political recrimination. In his position he had a good idea of the dangers and emotional dynamite of the Russian situation.

The *Hampshire* sailed at the appointed hour, in bad weather conditions, against naval advice, unescorted and on an unswept course out of northern Scotland. There is some evidence that a bomb was concealed among the stores on board and, when the ship's end came, it was reported by an eye witness that Kitchener declined to take to the boat, saying: "It is no use."

What had Cheiro told him? What was his *Fate* should he survive the peril at sea? The cold gray waves closed over all, and kept the secret. But Kitchener knew he was a doomed man and, from his actions, clearly preferred a clean break and a hero's end.

On the night of June 5, 1916, when the *Hampshire* was enduring her last grim struggle, Cheiro was sitting in the long music room of Henley house, discussing the war with friends when they were startled by a loud crash at the north end of the room. A big oaken shield, bearing the arms of Britain, lay broken on the floor. Cheiro noted the break, exactly between England and Ireland, and said: "This is an omen that some terrible blow has at this moment been dealt to England. I feel some naval disaster has taken place in which Ireland is in some way concerned."

When Cheiro learned of the *Hampshire's* loss, with Kitchener on board, his thoughts went back to that evening when it happened and he said the shield falling and breaking was Kitchener's way of fulfilling his promise to send Cheiro a sign.

At Henley house, more of the strange psychic manifestations that seemed to follow Cheiro wherever he went, took place. A famous medium was a house guest and was so relieved to escape from the noise and terror of the London air raids for a few days, that she uttered the wish that she, in turn, might be able to do something to show her gratitude.

As if in answer to her wish, the roses on the dinner table were lifted from their bowl by unseen hands and laid on the lace mats at each plate! Silence. Then the medium said: "It is a message from our spirit friends." She took it as a suggestion that a séance would be fruitful and after dinner, taking the roses with them, everyone went upstairs to a room reserved for séances and sat quietly in a circle.

The first supernatural visitor was a nurse, Edith Cavell, who wanted to prove to her skeptical doctor brother that the soul side of life goes on after the death of the material body. He was a friend of Cheiro and heard his sister's voice with his own ears. Edward VII also came and asked everyone present to pray for England. Cheiro's dear friend Nordice, the opera singer, showed up from the *Beyond* and charmed everyone with her glorious voice.

The séance came to a close. They went downstairs and discovered several local people in the garden who had been attracted from the roadway by the singing. They begged Cheiro to have the singer sing that song just once more. Cheiro told them that the singer had left.

Chapter Thirteen

Ireland and the "Troubles"

With the coming of war, horizons narrowed. No longer was it possible, either for business reasons or on a momentary whim, to cross oceans and continents merely by providing the fare. It had become a hazardous enterprise, surrounded by a network of documents, visas, and so on. No longer could you travel for pleasure; you had to plan such journeys with regard to their ultimate purpose, inconvenience and even the danger involved.

In 1917 Cheiro left for Ireland. He had official blessing to continue some experiments, which it was hoped would be fruitful in the war effort. These were in connection with the making of artificial coal from peat and activated carbon. It was thought that large-scale production would be useful both as fuel and as a necessary constituent in the masks that were being issued as protection against gas warfare!

By this time, Cheiro's income from the champagne business had been suspended because of the war. The *American Register* had died a fairly painless death due to the changed circumstances affecting British and American residents in Paris. In addition, it required little psychic ability to realize that any returns from his investment in Russian rails were gone with the overthrow of the Czar.

But Cheiro was not dismayed. He always had some new project underway and a tremendous capacity for turning his back on the past — however agreeable it might have been.

Taking a house in Dublin, where the peat experiments continued, he scanned the countryside for a suitable site to begin operations in earnest. It had to be near a peat bog so for months he lived in an old mansion at Tannamore, set in a huge park with a mile-long carriage drive from the main road.

The house was now a stately ruin, its interior a faded museum of relics of past grandeur, having been in the same family for centuries. The stone-paved banqueting hall, with its Crusader banners, tapestry, suits of armor and collections of various outlandish weapons, and its great carved stone fireplace topped with armorial bearings, recalled feudal days and was an ideal haunt for ghosts. These were not lacking and indeed were very turbulent; it being thought that they resented their descendants' poverty that forced them to put the place up for sale. Both the house and its massive fittings had associations with the Vale of Glendalonga in County Wicklow where there are ruins of the Seven Churches, symbolically connected with Rome's legendary seven hills.

The grand staircase lead from this hall to the floor above, divided into two branches at a half-landing, which looked onto a park and, in the distance beyond that, a lake. The main bedroom suites opened from the landing, each room more magnificent than the next — rooms with huge curtained four-posters, one provided with a step commode to reach the bed; massive ancient furniture that must have been built inside the rooms for it never could have gone through the double doors, which gave an air of ceremony to the lofty apartments.

The whole place was scantily illuminated by oil lamps or candles, so it was quite a nerve-wracking experience to travel the long, dark stretches when he sought out his own suite at night after dinner, until at last another oasis of friendly light was reached.

From the first day Cheiro arrived, he began to hear strange sounds. An old spinet suddenly emitted sweet, thin, faded music — but nobody was playing! In addition, every now and then, he saw the misty outline of a woman; the staircase paneling showing quite clearly through her full skirts and ruffles! Many a time they heard the sound of a coach and horses driving up to the front door in the dead of night, invisible horses pawing the pavement, wheels crunching against the gravel. Then, unfailingly came a scream — followed by a man's heavy tread on the stairs and the footsteps always went off down one of the long corridors to another wing.

One evening, two of the maids — greatly agitated — were running about desperately, came into Cheiro's suite and asked him to witness a most unusual spectacle. He went with the two trembling girls to a window overlooking the main courtyard. There, in the brilliant moonlight was a great crowd of frightened animals who had rushed there seeking sanctuary from an unseen foe.

Foxes, geese, pheasants and other wild birds and small furry beasts were all huddled together with the domestic animals and poultry! There was hardly a sound to be heard from these panic-stricken animals except for a few hushed cries, the bleating of lambs and the whimpering of the dogs.

Then, a low prolonged wailing came from outside in the park. And somebody cried: — 'It is the Element!'

Everyone, man and beast, seemed to realize that some primitive, bestial, elemental spirit was about, and the terror of this, submerged even the natural instinct of prey and predator among this strange assorted multitude. As the bloodcurdling wails came nearer, humans and animals cringed and trembled. Some of the men crossed themselves. Some were down on their knees. It was as if a blight had descended on the whole throng.

Suddenly, everybody noticed that Cheiro and one of the farmers were lighting an old cresset that stood on a low, flat roof nearby. They plied it with peat soaked in paraffin oil; someone nailed two pieces of wood together to form a cross and planted it in the heart of the blazing cresset. As it started to burn, Cheiro stepped forward like an exorcist, calling upon God to show mercy on this besieged place and praying for deliverance from this evil spirit.

As it appeared through an open window, the scene was almost medieval. The blazing cresset and flaming cross lit up Cheiro's tall, mysterious-looking figure. The dark red dressing gown became a priestly robe and his outstretched arms proclaimed a sacrificial attitude. Nearby huddled the praying women, as the moonlight illuminated the scared eyes and quivering, almost soundless motions of that great crowd of birds and beasts below, while round them surged that bitter, eerie wailing.

Gradually the wailing faded, as one by one the animals slipped quietly away and a sense of peace came to everyone, who silently returned to their own place, perhaps to pray!

It was an uncanny experience — even for a seer. For a time there was no disturbance...until one night — the phantom coach returned!

This time, the heavy footsteps came on and paused right at Cheiro's door! He tried not to be frightened but he was rigid! Something shook the door violently! — He heard a horrible laugh.... Then came the crash of breaking glass, followed by a sickening thud on the gravel below. He could only conclude that the ghost had thrown himself out of the landing window!

Two days later, Cheiro and Mena, who had also shared this terrible experience, left Tannamore forever. "Too haunted for us!" the couple was heard to say.

They found a place to live in an old rambling mansion near a large stretch of peat bog. The Count started making preparations to build his factory, while making the house habitable. It was in a very run down condition. Water was brought in, lights installed; a great deal of work was done while they stayed at a hotel in the village of Tullamore.

Before deciding where to settle, they inspected many estates, several of them in semi-derelict condition. One of these was Gortnamona, which was in ruins and of which many strange tales were told. Driving over with the agent, he was told about a tragedy that happened there forty years before, which had given the place its bad name.

The house was occupied at the time by a young Squire, a wild-type by all accounts, and his fascinating young wife, of whom he was possessively, almost pathologically jealous. One night they were entertaining a large house party and, following a great banquet, the wife was murdered, lamps were overturned — setting fire to the mansion and completely destroying it along with any possible clues as to how the murder was committed.

There were many casualties, the Squire lost his sanity and for the rest of his life dwelt in the house of his steward, on the estate. He ordered the gates of the domain to be shut. In the high-walled meadows of the park, the cattle were turned loose to roam at will. When the estate passed to his next of kin in the United States twenty years later, he ordered the cattle to be slaughtered and the estate sold. But although the estate agents persevered and took many people to see it, no one ever bought it.

Local people believed that leprechauns inhabited the overgrown glades and avenues, and that banshees wailed mournfully throughout the ruins. *Nature*, left to her own devices, had created a portrait of sylvan beauty, carpeting the approaches with ferns, moss and wild flowers, and screening the harsh ruins with climbing roses and bright creepers, through which the broken stoneworks that contained mica, sparkled in the sun. Trees had taken root in the walls and in the vast ovens of the bake-house there still remained charred loaves of bread. The very air seemed stilled; time had stood still, awaiting the touch of the wand that would end this fairytale bewitchment and bring all to life again. Nothing could have created a greater contrast than the beauty with which *Nature* had enveloped this scene, coupled with the gruesome drama of its human story that was sufficient to repel intruders for so many years, and transformed the whole place into a thing of sheer haunted enchantment.

The peasantry was a strange mixture of fatalism, superstition, whimsical humor, courage and stubborn though sometimes misplaced loyalty. Fantastic tales were told, and interminable discussions went on about the most outlandish problems with perfect seriousness until, just as it seemed that either they or the rest of the world were crazy, a concluding quirk in their word or voice tone indicated that they might not believe all they were saying.

One morning Bridget, the cook, asked the handyman:

'Patrick, an' what time be 6 o'clock? Be it 5 o'clock or 7 o'clock?'

"Pat gazed at the sun, like a duck looking up at a crown, and called back, 'Och, an' how would I be knowing? For sure, both be wrong! Now isn't' it that one half of the year it's too soon and t'other half it's too late? And for meself, I consult the ould sundial. For the ould divils in the Parlimint can't be meddling with the sun himself, bedad, being himself out of reach!'

'Then how will I be calling his honor at 6 o'clock?' persisted Bridget.

'Now, don't ye be minding about that 'avourneen, for if ye call him too soon, it serves him right! An' if ye call him too late, sure he'll only have himself to blame, an' he in Parlimint will be after seeing what a muck they make wid their meddling!'

"Having settled this problem to his own liking and without riposte from Bridget, he took out his jew's harp and went briskly off playing a rebel air 'as swately an' softly as a drame,' with Bridget flinging after him a parting benediction — so as to have the last word...."

At last they moved into their own home. Having sent over from London a large shipment of furniture, they were busy for months making their surroundings as comfortable as possible. Meanwhile, Cheiro was engrossed in getting his factory built. Men and lads from the village were employed; peat was cut and dried before making it into bricks for the winter fuel supply.

Interested in getting the home farm going, two hundred eggs a day were being collected from the poultry, which had been provided with modern poultry houses. Geese roamed the meadow, and a good number of turkeys were raised. After the state of semi-starvation they had endured in London in the latter years of the War, it was a joy for them to sit at a table and enjoy such simple things as home-made bread and butter from their own dairy, garnished with their own garden produce. They had abundance, and to spare, and gratefully shared it with those less fortunate.

Experiments went steadily on and production began to mount, but, along with other residents in Ireland in those troubled times, they were subjected to repeated annoyance and even danger by the protagonists of this other war within a war.

Long planks were always lashed to the car when Cheiro and Mena went out so that they could cross some ditch that was cut across the road. There were many hold-ups and experience warned them not to touch any object lying on the road, since many mines were laid. This made them very cautious. One time they were driving down a long, narrow country lane when they saw -- straight ahead -- a big, knobby sack. There was no room to go round it, so their driver stopped and went along to look it over from a respectful distance.

When they joined him, he said: "Sure, and it can't be a dead body, for never did a corpse have so many spikes sticking up on it."

There were no wires attached to it that they could see, and they discovered that it was three heavy sacks stitched together and well filled. But with what? They decided they could not go round it and the road was too narrow to turn around so the only thing to do was to move the obstacle and drive on!

"'Ah, well," said Dan the driver. "It's a coward that I am, but praise be to God, I can only die once! Now, Count, you take your lady back to the car and cover yourselves up with the rug in case of glass splinters, for it's meself that's going to remove whatever the thing is!"

Cheiro and Mena returned to the car where they covered themselves with the rug. After a few minutes, they heard a great shout and peals of laughter. Dan, who had watched them get into the car so fearfully, was brandishing the stick with which he had tickled the monster — holding up a gleaming golden church candlestick and crucifix. "Loot!" he cried jubilantly.

They piled the sack of booty rifled from the church into the car and headed for the nearest police barracks.

When using the car, they always made sure to have two flags, one British and the other Sinn Fein; also a bottle of whiskey, bandages and iodine. Many times they came in handy when they were stopped. They always tried to be neutral. The British soldiers were always well behaved and hated the Black and Tans, because, they said: "They disgraced the King's uniform."

Sometimes they found someone lying on the roadside, badly wounded and bleeding to death. Often they would take the victim back to their house where Mena dressed his wounds and they gave him shelter until he was able to get to his home on his own. Of course, this was very risky, but they felt they couldn't let a fellow lie there to perish.

The men on Cheiro's estate made a hospital ward inside a large turf building. There was a small wooden shed with three or four camp beds in it, an electric light and an airshaft. Outside, peat turf was stacked and slabs of turf were nailed on the door, as well as loose blocks piled to hide the entrance. It was so well done that no one could tell it concealed a hospital shed. This turf rick was nearest the house, and Cheiro or Mena could slip through the enclosed outer courtyard at night without being seen, late at night — sometimes all night, if there was a very bad casualty.

This tiny hospital temporarily housed some of the most daring fighters of the Civil War. The house was raided dozens of times, but the police and Black and Tans never found the hospital. Michael Collins passed this way many times to visit wounded comrades, as did Rory O'Connor, another famous rebel with a price on his head!

In the male servants quarters they also had, for a time, a very badly wounded Black and Tan who was released from Strangeways Gaol for murdering his wife and allowed to come over to Ireland to kill the Irish — and get paid for it! They found him in a ditch not far from the gates. He was carried up to the house and laid on the table of the servants' back kitchen. He had a flesh wound all down one of his legs, from hip to ankle and a bullet wound in his right hand.

A bed was prepared for him in the men's dormitory, but not without some grumbling on their part. The wounded man was undressed and placed on a sheet; he was given an injection, his wounds were cleaned, dressed and stitched. The cut had been made by a scythe and was over a yard long. This Lancashire man told some horrific stories and confessed that he would rather be back in Strangeways Gaol. He had had enough of this Civil War.

But before he was well enough to be moved, there was a nasty raid by the Black and Tans who ordered everyone out in the yard. When they came across their comrade he told them to go easy, as he had been so well treated. That evening they took him away; he was sorry to leave.

This period, with the big war now mercifully ended, but the small one continuing as bitter and malignant as ever, is criss-crossed with the activity of the factory and laboratories and the even more feverish humanitarian efforts to pursue an equitable and humane course, even though it meant circumventing authority.

This kind of thing had to be faced every day, while trying to make a living: killing and being killed! And yet the devout rebels could not bear to miss Mass. But if they attended openly, it could be the equivalent of suicide. This was not too much for human ingenuity. Cellars were frequently used for services. One Sunday, a raid was made on a chapel while a service was in progress. The sanctity of a holy place was invoked by the offenders and all guns were hastily left on the floor.

Going into the kitchen one morning, Cheiro found a sack of flour there, with a note on the table asking that it be made into bread. There was bustling and hustling in the kitchen all through the night and rows of crisp loaves awaited the soft-footed prowlers who came and collected their food in the gray dawn.

The raiders seemed infallibly to choose the most inconvenient times for their visits, such as in the dead of night when everyone would have to parade sleepily in their thin night attire. Some of the most exacting raids took place during Cheiro's occasional visits to Wamyas Castle.

It was also dangerous to have cash lying around. Near the end of their stay in Ireland, they held an auction sale and needed a place to hide the money until they could get it to the bank. Cheiro crumpled wads of notes inside balls of old newspaper, which were carelessly tossed into the waste-paper basket. Sure enough, a raid took place. 'Where is the money?' they wanted to know. Cheiro disclaimed any knowledge of it or its whereabouts as they ransacked the whole house.

The only place they didn't search was the waste-paper basket! That night Cheiro retrieved the notes, wrapped them carefully in greaseproof paper and oilskin, popped them into a thermos flask and filled it with thick, cold custard. Next morning, after an adventurous journey, he entered the bank in triumph and looked about for a flowerpot in which to empty the custard before he could remove the money, little the worse for its passage.

On another occasion, one of their maids, a good girl who came from a village some distance away, came asking, unexpectedly, if she might have that day off. She seemed rather worried so Cheiro asked if there was anything wrong.

Her mother, it seems, was bedridden and the neighbor who looked after her was also ill, so her mother would be alone and uncared for and the maid needed to go home.

"'Better than that," said Cheiro. "I will take you there in the car. That will be quicker and we can take along a few things for her. Come with me to the kitchen and let's see what cook can give us."

As they entered the little cabin, they saw that a local nun had looked in to cheer up the old woman and tidy up the place. While the nun was lighting a fire and as she saw the flames dancing upward and felt the comforting warmth steal into her bones, the bright-eyed old woman gleefully exclaimed, with no other thought of anything but gratitude: "Sure, and it's a fine blaze that we've made, glory be to St. Patrick! And may fire everlasting be wid ye!!"

The nun gave a gentle smile, and no one mentioned how inappropriate such a reward would be to one of her calling.

Chapter Fourteen

Farewell to Erin

And so life went on for the Hamons until 1922. In 1919 Cheiro had entered into an agreement with Colonel Clibborn, which granted him rights over an area of 173 acres of the Bog of Allen. A lot of money was spent on developing this locale to drain it, open up roads, etc., and a large factory with its special plant and machinery was now in place to manufacture the new peat fuel on an commercial scale. Now that World War I was over, the use of activated carbon for gas masks had lapsed, though its greater employment for other scientific purposes was increasing.

This fuel, when subjected to the Hamon process, was said in various scientists' reports, to almost equal coal in its heat-producing power. It had the appearance of a coal briquette, was cleaner than coal to handle, burnt with a good flame - without the danger of sparks, left little ash and no clinker. It withstood transport and it was manufactured automatically, with each press easily maintaining an output of one ton per hour. The finished fuel block was automatically carried on a travelling belt to trucks or to storage, thus reducing unnecessary labor and handling. The manufacture being carried out above ground, the danger and potentially disastrous conditions of coal mining were avoided, and healthy and productive employment was secured for large numbers of men in the district.

Since this bog alone was estimated to contain about four million tons of peat easily available for extraction, and with many other bogs readily accessible nearby, the prospects once more looked rosy for the Count's fortunes. Several prominent scientists, including Sir Oliver Lodge, Sir W.F. Barrett, and Prof. Benton, had personally endorsed the new fuel, whose manufacture incidentally also included many new by-products.

Everything was in good shape for a big push and everybody discounted the political upheavals that for so long had been an annoyance and an interruption to normal working activities. This was just something extra to be coped with and taken in stride; part of the local condition, as an unpleasant climate, troublesome insects or a hostile tribe might be elsewhere.

But it is never safe to assume that the human element is stable, especially in Ireland. Louis Hamon was Irish by birth and had brought some measure of prosperity to the district in which they were working. Yet when political passions rose high, that fact did not protect his property, nor preserve the livelihood of the fellow countrymen he was striving to benefit. Cheiro had overcome his early aversion to his homeland now that he could achieve what he wanted in his own environment and be both usefully and profitably occupied. He began hoping he could make a permanent home in this dear, distressful country.

The prophecy, made over thirty years ago by the old Egyptian, was fulfilled — that during a Great War he would find himself once again living in Ireland. But Cheiro had forgotten the other part of that prophecy, that *Fate* had decreed he would never have a home for any length of time.

So they survived the troublesome period when Sinn Fein was actively fighting against England, leading up to the formation of the Irish Free State and the Treaty of 1929. But then the Irish began fighting among themselves! And one night the Republicans burned down his factory to try to force the employees to join their side.

Cheiro and Mena looked at the damage and wept.... It was certainly no time for argument and it was no use crying over spilt milk. It was impossible to rebuild and start up again. The plant was utterly destroyed and the factory gutted. They expected ultimately to receive compensation for the extensive damage and loss of production, but obviously that time was not now.

Without dwelling on the past, they decided to go back to London and started dismantling the house so that the remaining furniture and effects could be packed and sent on. The last object to be included was the mummy's hand. Cheiro would, of course, take this with him personally in the same way as he had faithfully done since it had come into his trusteeship — all those years before.

The hand sat, on its ebony stand and purple velvet cushion, in the salon. The protection promised Cheiro by the Egyptian when the hand was transferred into his keeping had certainly been extended to him. Once, a thief in Chicago dropped his spoils and fled in terror on coming in contact with those stony fingers in the darkness. On another occasion, in South America, the hotel where he was staying caught fire.

Everyone rushed to escape — but Cheiro, while listening with the others for the approach of the elevator, suddenly remembered he had forgotten the mummy's hand! So much was this a part of his life that he instantly went back to retrieve it, leaving the others to crowd into the waiting elevator. Its ropes burned in the roof and the elevator crashed to the ground — killing everybody in it!

He had these and many other instances to recall, with respect, before he made any hasty decisions regarding this traveling companion. But some months before the burning of the factory in Ireland, a strange metamorphosis occurred. The hand, formerly as rigid as ebony, began to soften and become pliable. Drops of dark, red liquid appeared on the knuckles and oozed from the fingertips! He called in a chemist who worked in the factory.

"Have you ever heard of a mummy's hand, for that matter any part of a mummy showing signs of bleeding after being embalmed for over 3,000 years?" he asked.

"Never!" was the reply. "Such a thing would be impossible — and absolutely unbelievable!"

"Well," returned Cheiro. "Do you see this mummy's hand lying on that cushion? You will remember, when you came here in 1920, it was as hard and as rigid as if carved out of a piece of oak. You can see, now, that the flesh has become soft and the fingers supple, and what appears to be dark, red blood is now oozing from the fingers. Take it into the laboratory and analyze a drop of the liquid under the microscope, and give me your opinion. After that, use every means you have at your disposal to restore the hand to its former hardness and rigid condition."

A few hours later, the chemist reported there could be no doubt that it was human blood oozing from the fingers. He added that the only thing he could do to stop the bleeding and restore it to its former rigid state was to dip the entire hand in a solution of pitch and shellac.

The chemist furnished a sworn affidavit to prove his statement, and one was also given by the manager of the factory who witnessed, not without a certain shrinking interest, his experiments in the efforts made to restore the hand to its former condition. For a while, the solution stopped the bleeding. The hand appeared as before and was returned to its resting place in the salon, reposing, once again, on its cushion.

But then the blood again began to seep, forcing its way through the coating of pitch and shellac. The hand itself became soft and showed signs of melting away. Cheiro didn't know what to do! He felt bound to keep it with him, yet how could he? Pictures of all kinds of predicaments — with customs and police — filled his head.

At last, nothing remained in the salon but the hand. One night, four thieves made a violent entry into the room. As they arrogantly switched on the lights, the ring of Egyptian gold on the first finger of the hand caught their attention. The leader snatched at it — but dropped it at once on finding his own hand covered with blood! Cursing out of fright, he rushed out of the house with his comrades hot on his heels!

A few nights later, realizing the hand couldn't be taken with him because of its condition, he decided to cremate it. They lit a large fire in the hall that it might be consigned to the flames.

It happened by purest chance to be Halloween, the last night of October, when, it is believed, the spirits of the dead come back to visit their friends. It was a radiant, moonlit, calm night. Cheiro and Mena sauntered through the garden, observing for the last time, the mountains of Tipperary rearing themselves to the sky some twenty miles to the south. Their conversation naturally turned to Egypt, picturing the ancient tombs of Thebes, and recalling the scene when the mummy's hand was passed over to him. And now he remembered: "At the end of a great war, this hand will attempt to get free from your custody; and the 'Ka,' or spirit, imprisoned in it will return to its own."

As they turned to go into the house to perform the final act of liberation for the long-gone princess, they noticed that the servants had left the dining room windows open, with a supper on the table, following the Irish custom of bidding welcome to the spirits of the departed on that one night of the year.

Then they remembered it was Halloween. They closed and bolted the outer porch and the heavy oak doors of the inner hall, sat on empty packing cases in the bright firelight, and prepared to bid farewell to what almost seemed like an old friend.

Cheiro had a look of sadness and suggested that perhaps some prayer should be offered: "After all, her God, for

135

all we know, may have been our own, only under a different name."

He then quoted a verse from the Egyptian Book of the Dead.

Thy flesh have I given unto thee,
Thy bones have I kept for thee,
Thy members have I collected.
Thou art set in order,
Thou seest the Gods,
Thou settest out on thy way.
Thine hand reaches beyond the horizon and
Unto the holy place where thou wouldst be.

As the whispered words died away, Cheiro slipped the ebony stand, the velvet cushion and the hand into the heart of the flames. The instant they touched the fire -- long, white brilliant tongues of silvery flames shot upward and the odor of the embalming spices filled the room. Wordlessly, a little sadly, they watched until all was consumed.

Suddenly, they heard a noise like a whirlwind at the doors of the outer porch. A similar pressure was exerted on the stout, oaken, inner doors. The night was perfectly still and calm, and their only thought was of raiders, of which they had lately seen so many. With a last supreme effort, whoever was outside flung the doors open —! Nothing. No armed men entered.

Only bright moonlight flooded the hall, almost to where they stood. A cold shiver of presentiment passed over them as they gazed at the glass-enclosed porch. Something was taking shape. Gathering form as it came, it was wafting towards them, and in the contrasting shadow of the hall they could see the figure of a woman, every lineament marked with grandeur and pride. The head-dress, shaped like the wings of beetles, had the glint of beaten gold and flowed gracefully down to her slender shoulders. On her forehead, over the deep-set, inscrutable eyes, was a golden asp, emblem of Egyptian royalty, and an enormous scarab at her waist, fastened her jeweled girdle. The figure glided to where the fire had been, bent over it, then, rising, faced Cheiro and Mena with both hands clasped together.

Her lips seemed to move and they thought she was going to speak...her eyes looked into theirs. Then, throwing her head back, she lifted her hands slowly in an arch above her head, bowed towards them and glided backward through the hall and out onto the porch. As if bewitched, they followed, only to see the figure begin to float out into the night, becoming more nebulous, second by second, until only an impression of those glorious eyes remained, looking deep into theirs.

Deserted and bare, the hall faced them as they once more turned indoors, feeling emptied by the intense drama of the scene they had just witnessed. When dawn came, they raked out the ashes and gathered together the calcined bones of the hand, vowing that some day, somehow, they would strive to take them back to Egypt and place them in one of the tombs in the Valley of the Kings.

Alas, this opportunity never offered itself. The bones of the Princess' hand continued to watch over them for the rest of their days. They took the ancient Egyptian ring that was untarnished by the fire, gently rubbed the ashes from it, and kept it as a memento of that long and loyal companionship.

The night before they left the house, they were warned by men from the rebel army to be sure to leave before the following afternoon because they intended to destroy the railway bridges, and no more trains would be able to run to Dublin.

When they boarded the train the next day, the only carriage they could get was a Pullman behind the engine. It was filled with officers and soldiers from the new Irish Free Army. They were armed to the teeth and told Cheiro they were being drafted to Dublin where an attack by the rebels was expected that night. The soldiers helped them stow their valises on the luggage racks. Right above them they put a glass jar containing the bones from the mummy's hand.

The train pulled out and they made themselves as comfortable as possible for the sixty mile journey. The few civilians were, like them, also leaving Ireland. The rest of the train was packed with soldiers who livened-up the trip with Irish songs.

Suddenly, Cheiro was jerked into wakefulness by seeing Mena's eyes staring intently at the valise above his head. He looked up and saw its label shaking violently, in contrast to the gentle swaying of the other bags. On an impulse, Cheiro jumped to his feet and moved all their luggage to the floor! Scarcely had he done this and while the soldiers were still grumbling and asking why, the train lurched to a violent stop and all other baggage was thrown from the racks, injuring several passengers.

All was confusion! When they managed to struggle to the window, they could see the cause of the sudden halt. The station they were about to enter was on fire and parts of the roof were already falling onto the engine. The place was Liffey Junction, the last station on the line.

But a greater danger confronted them. Far away in the distance, they could hear the roar of an engine travelling at full speed — rushing towards them on the same track! Every fraction of a second it rushed nearer — tearing like a mad bull under a full head of steam! Everyone was stunned! Paralyzed with fright! Some men threw themselves on their knees and prayed while others white as death — seemed turned to stone!

The rebels had uncoupled the express engine of the Galway Mail train, pulled open the throttle and hurled it against the passengers, soldiers and civilians -- on their train!!

It seemed as though nothing could save them. Escape seemed impossible. And then a miracle happened. Was it *Chance* that caused the railway points to swing across, a hundred yards ahead — sending the swaying monster to the other track where it careened on — smashing through a freight train on the siding and crashing against a concrete wall?

They took their luggage and walked into Dublin, taking a cab across the city to the Kingstown train and caught the boat for England that night, the only passengers to do so....

On their arrival in London, the papers were full of Howard Carter's discovery of the steps leading to the tomb of *Tut-Ankh-Amen* in the *Valley of the Kings* in Egypt and they observed that the date of this discovery was the day after Cheiro and Mena cremated the hand of his sister.

A few weeks later, they were sitting in Cheiro's study in London, discussing the finding of the tomb and talking about Lord Carnarvon, who financed the search and was going to Egypt for the opening ceremony. The headlines read: "*Howard Carter Discovers Steps to Tomb of King Tut!*"

Cheiro was writing and Mena was finishing a pencil sketch of the Princess as she had appeared to them in the hall of their old Irish house. Then they noticed that in spite of a good fire, the room grew cold and the lamp on the writing table dimmed to a dull red glow. They looked at each other without speaking. In the gloom, they saw the now familiar form of the Princess taking shape! Her right hand was raised and seemed to be pointing to the writing pad in front of Cheiro. He seized a pencil and rapidly wrote down words that came to his mind. He seemed to be acting under dictation.

The vision faded, the light resumed its former power, and he read aloud what he had jotted down on the pad.... It warned Lord Carnarvon not to allow any of the relics found in the tomb to be removed. If he did, he would suffer an injury while in the tomb — a sickness from which he would not recover, and death would claim him in Egypt.

This warning was sent to Lord Carnarvon, reaching him, as he was about to leave England. He read it to the Hon. Richard Bethell and to a close friend of Admiral Smith Dorrien, who later related the incident.

Admitting he was deeply impressed by the warning, Lord Carnarvon said: "At this moment of my life, if all the mummies in Egypt were to warn me, I would go on with my project just the same."

Of course, it's well known that he did take relics out of the tomb and sent them to England; in fact, just about anything that wasn't nailed down! He would have taken still more if the Egyptian government hadn't intervened. He had his moment of triumph, all the newspapers praising his enterprise. And then one day in the tomb, an insect stung him on the cheek, blood poisoning set in and in spite of all that the doctors could do, he died a short distance away from the splendid tomb his great wealth had caused to be rediscovered.

Chance or *Fate*? Call it what you will, but can you wonder that they felt rewarded by their miraculous tenure of the mummy's hand, and that the late Countess Mena Hamon, until old age, infirmity and eventually death overtook her, persisted in attempting to restore even those calcined bones to their original home?

Chapter Fifteen

Business as Usual

Another of Cheiro's business ventures was following its familiar pattern. As usual it started on what seemed firm foundations, an original yet practical scheme, scientifically vouched for, illustriously sponsored. It gathered momentum, soared ahead — maintaining its altitude for awhile — then swooped dramatically, tragically, downwards towards extinction. No matter how sound these deals appeared initially, or how gilt-edged they had been for years before his arrival, they always seemed, afterwards, to come to grief.

For him, the slogan 'business as usual' meant enthusiasm, hard work, the promise of success — then, never-failing setbacks and loss. But where Count Hamon failed, Cheiro invariably succeeded.

They took a large house near Regents Park and resumed their customary London life. Although many of the notabilities of Victorian days whom Cheiro had known so well, were no more, other friends of pre-war days, also getting back into peace-time rhythm after the violent interruption of war, were eager to welcome him back. Cheiro seemed as much in demand as ever, though the extreme degree of concentration that his profession demanded exacted an ever-increasing penalty on his health.

Countess Hamon's son, Jack, by her ill-fated first marriage, predicted so long ago by Cheiro, had been with them intermittently in Ireland. They had been forced, in the boy's best interests, to send him elsewhere for the strange reason that he always kept his hands in his pockets! This was a very dangerous thing to do in Ireland. Everyone was so trigger-happy in those uncertain times that concealing your hands was deemed a sure prelude to producing a gun — and using it! In those circumstances a person was liable to shoot first and ask questions later. This happened to Jack at least once, and fortunately, it only resulted in a hole in his hat.

His mother deemed it wiser not to risk further provocation, for she knew, no matter how often he was warned, he would sooner or later forget and repeat the offence. He was a highly-strung, temperamental young man, very fond of Cheiro but a little jealous of his place in her affections. Having a talent for music, he continued his education in Dublin and later enrolled at the Royal Academy of Music, where he studied under many notable names in the music world, eventually becoming assistant organist for a period at Brompton Oratory, where he was a great favorite. As time went on, he showed promise of becoming a good concert pianist — and a particularly fine interpreter of Chopin.

To give Cheiro the rest and change that were essential to him and beneficial to the entire household, they took a house in Jersey in the summer of 1923 and retained it for several years. Everyone enjoyed the splendid scenery, climate and relaxation and kept putting off returning until one day a telegram arrived from the butler at their house in London, saying that a Hindu had camped out on the steps leading to the front door and refused to move until he saw Cheiro. The man claimed he was acting for his master, an Indian maharajah, who was staying at the Claridge Hotel.

Taking the next boat back to London, Cheiro soon found the problem he was asked to decide: what should the maharajah do about his camel corps? An astrologer had foretold that India would be invaded by Russia and he and the other friendly princes were ready to make a big gesture on Indian defense to the Raj and his government.

Around this time, the future of Cheiro's peat coal project again took a turn for the better. He was associated with several big financiers. The Artificial Coal Co. (Hamon Process), Ltd., with an authorized share capital of one hundred and twenty pounds, was formed. It was actually incorporated in Jersey, to save taxes, but it was to operate in Ireland where Cheiro still retained the rights granted to him over part of the Bog of Allen. Once again, all went well for a time, and then Cheiro was made to believe he had grounds to mistrust some of his associates. He withdrew from the board and after his resignation, his suspicions were confirmed. In the resultant confusion he decided not to sink any more money into the scheme and it was abandoned.

In 1924, illness struck again, and this time it was Mena. She was miraculously cured of asthma, a thirty-year affliction, by the then little practiced treatment of gold ionization. But then she was brought down by pneumonia. While lying there, struggling back towards health, word was brought to her that the Count had collapsed in a taxi that was taking him to some business appointment, and he had only just succeeded in bribing the driver to take him home rather than to a hospital.

He lay in a coma. Doctors were called in and diagnosed a slight stroke. A considerable quantity of blood was taken from him which somewhat relieved the congestion, but then he, too, got another bout of pneumonia.

When he began to recover, a sea voyage was recommended, but he was as weak as a kitten and couldn't stand the hustle and bustle which usually preceded a long journey.

Mena arranged to have him transferred by ambulance to a cargo vessel that was making a leisurely voyage to the United States, via South America and the Panama Canal. Luggage was packed, their Rolls Royce crated and taken aboard, followed by two creaking passengers clad in pneumonia jackets, who went straight to bed as soon as they reached the ship.

It was a marvelous voyage, and upon their return, the doctors scarcely recognized their patients, so thorough had been their recuperation.

However, an unpleasant experience was now waiting for Cheiro. A claim had been made against his company for compensation of twelve thousand, nine hundred and sixty pounds because of the destruction of the peat works at Ballycumber in August 1922 during the civil war. The case came up for hearing before County Court Judge Roche at Dublin Castle, the respondents being the Ministry of Finance. Mr. W. G. Shannon, and Mr. Walter Callan, instructed by Messrs. Hoey and Denning, acted for the claimants, Mr. Lupton, and Mr. C. Davitt, instructed by Mr. James Rogers, State Solicitors, represented the government.

The claim was fiercely contested and the defendants endeavored by every means within their power to discredit Cheiro. They sneered at his profession and commented sardonically on the strangely consistent ill luck that had attended his business projects.

A fairly full newspaper account of the proceedings gives some idea of the ordeal all this involved:

"...Count Louis Le Warner Hamon, managing director of the firm, gave evidence. Describing the visit of three armed and masked men to his residence after the burning in November, 1922, he said that the spokesman of the party said: 'I am very sorry, Count, that we have to come like this and annoy you, but our orders must be obeyed, and we have been sent here tonight to tell you that if you persist in making any attempt to save the machinery at the burned down factory, you will cause some of your men to be shot, and if you still insist further, we will then have to burn you out at Prospect, as well.'

"The witness then said he argued with the man and said what a shame it was to throw so many men out of work since he had only closed down temporarily until things got better. The reply he got was that the men had thought only of their bellies and were no good to the raiders. He asked for a chance to save some of the machinery but the man replied that it did not suit their plans, saying: 'The more damage we can do, the more this alien government with the English government at their back will have to pay in the end. So I give you fair warning, if you make any attempt to save any of these machines or parts of the factory, we are very sorry for you, but we will burn you out altogether.'

"The men then went away and we thought the best thing would be to have an auction of the farm stock and get out of Ireland as fast as we could."

Mr. Callan: 'Did you sell your furniture?'

Cheiro: 'We sent the furniture back to England.'

Mr. Callan: 'After that, did you take any steps to try to protect the machines of the factory?'

Cheiro: 'No. We left Prospect on the 7th of November, 1922.'

"The witness further said they were desirous of restarting the factory at Ballycumber.

"In the course of cross-examination by Mr. Lupton, the witness said he could not say that it was Irregulars who destroyed the factory. He asked who they were, and they said they were the Irish Republican Army

Mr. Lupton: 'Did the Irregulars or Republican Army help you at the auction?'

Cheiro: 'Yes, they did help me. We were being looted by a gang and the Irish Republican Army came to the rescue with revolvers.'

Mr. Lupton: 'They wanted to injure the government and not to injure you?'

Cheiro: 'I believe so. I don't think they wanted to injure me.'

"Replying to further questions, Cheiro said he was a large shareholder in the factory and had fifty thousand shares out of a total of one hundred and twenty thousand.

Questioned as to the beginning of the factory, he said he was approached by the late Mr. Joseph Nolan, M.P. He came to Ireland in 1917 and was studying this artificial peat fuel. The factory started in 1919. Mr. Nolan had been trying to get money from the British government to start a factory in Ireland.

"Counsel put several questions as to what business the witness had carried on before, and he said that for about seventeen years he had a large champagne business in France; he had newspapers in France and London; he traveled as a financier to Russia and other places; and before that he was principally a writer and author. He had been a director of several companies.

"Questioned particularly about a Threadneedle Syndicate, he said he had been a director of it. It was formed to deal with all kinds of general merchants.

Mr. Lupton: 'Did it purport to supply shells for the European War?'

Cheiro: 'Yes, they did all sorts of things.'

Mr. Lupton: 'Was a Baron Oppenheim also connected with the company?'

"He believed the Baron was dead. Mr. Lupton put some questions to the witness as to his name, and he said his name was Louis William Le Warner Hamon.

Mr. Lupton: 'I put it to you that your name is not Hamon, but Warner.'

Cheiro: 'My name is Hamon!'

"Counsel produced a baptismal certificate and put it to witness that he was christened William John Warner.

"The witness said he supposed that was the proper certificate; and went on to say he was born in Bray Co., Dublin, in 1866. His father discovered he was entitled to the name Le Warner and traced his family back to their marriage into the Hamons of Normandy. The witness took out by deed poll the name Louis Le Warner Hamon, or Count Hamon.

"Answering other questions, the witness said he was also known by the name of Cheiro, and explained that it was a *nom de plume* under which he wrote. He had published a book entitled Cheiro's Memoirs, in 1912.

Mr. Lupton: 'Did you state in that book that you took up the study of palmistry and devoted your life to the study?'

Cheiro: 'I did, up to that time.'

Mr. Lupton: 'You spent a large part of your time as a palmist in London?'

Cheiro: 'I did, and all over the world.'

Mr. Lupton: 'You were not candid when you did not tell me anything about this precarious occupation of palmist.'

Cheiro: 'There was nothing precarious about it; I earned more money than most of you barristers.' (Laughter).

"The witness added that this was before the period that counsel had been asking him about:

Mr. Lupton: 'Was Baron Oppenheim living in the house where you were acting as palmist?'

Cheiro: 'Absolutely not!'

Mr. Lupton: 'If the police made that report against you, would it be true?'

Cheiro: 'Absolutely not.'

"Mr. Lupton showed the witness a photograph and asked if it was a photograph of him, and witness replied that it was.

"Counsel said it was a photograph given to them by the authorities of Scotland Yard, London, along with a report.

The Judge: 'You have no right to state to me that you have a report from Scotland Yard, but you can put questions. The statement made by Scotland Yard — unless you are going to bring someone over to prove it — should not be mentioned at all.'

Cheiro: 'Have I committed any crime that I should come here to hear a report of Scotland Yard read?'

"Questioned as to a bank in Paris, the witness said he had been connected with it but he denied that any proceedings were instituted against him by the French authorities in respect of his dealings with it:

Mr. Lupton: 'Did two American ladies complain to the police that they were defrauded of five hundred and twenty thousand francs?'

Cheiro: 'Yes, but many clients might make complaints.'

Mr. Lupton: 'In consequence of this, were you arrested by the French authorities?'

Cheiro: 'I never was; your information is completely wrong.'

Mr. Lupton: 'Perhaps it is.... Were you ever brought before the French authorities on a charge of having defrauded two American ladies of five hundred and twenty thousand francs?'

Cheiro: 'I was never brought up in respect of any such charge.'

Cheiro added: 'Any person might make a complaint. The Judge was only asked to investigate it. He sent for me, investigated it, and I never heard anymore about it.'

Mr. Lupton: 'You were before him on that charge?'

Cheiro: 'Just as hundreds of others were before him.'

Mr. Lupton: 'Did you leave France after that charge was made?'

Cheiro: 'I remained nearly nine months, and left in the ordinary routine.'

Mr. Lupton: 'Were you fined five hundred pounds and sentenced to thirteen months imprisonment on that charge, in your absence?'

Cheiro: 'In my absence, I believe, the case was never tried and never came before the Courts…. You are dealing with French law, which is very different.'

"Asked whether from March 1906 to 1908 he carried on the business of a company in Gracechurch Street, London, he said it was carried on in his name by a man named Hugo Lowy.

Mr. Lupton: 'Had you a financial interest in that business?

Cheiro: 'I put money in it.'

Mr. Lupton: 'And you were getting profits?'

Cheiro: 'I never got any profits.'

"Among other matters he was asked about a company called Oil Processes, Ltd., and said he was never connected with it. It went into liquidation. With regard to a company called Flax, Ltd., he was a director of it, and it financed Oil Processes, Ltd.

Mr. Lupton: 'It went into liquidation?'

Cheiro: 'It finally went into liquidation eighteen months after I resigned.'

"Counsel called attention to a description of witness as *Comte* and the witness answered, 'My title of *Comte* is the French title — the Norman title.'

"Replying finally to questions about the factory in Offay, he said they were not able to deliver the produce to the public on account of the troubled condition of the country, and it was a great sorrow that the factory was burned, otherwise they would be making money and employing a lot of men.

146

"In re-examination by Mr. Callan, he said he put a large sum of money into the industry of getting fuel from peat:

Mr. Callan: 'And it has gone up in smoke?'

Cheiro: 'Yes.'

"He also said that the condition of the country prevented orders from being carried out. The claim was supported by particulars supplied to the Government as to how the items were made up.

"The witness further said, in reference to an incident in France that was referred to, that he had been interrogated by the magistrate after it was suggested that there had been a fraud perpetrated against some ladies. He remained eight or nine months in France after that and the ladies did get their money back. They had invested in shares and, during the American panic, these shares had to be pledged to raise money for these ladies.

Cheiro: 'We bought them back,' he added, 'and delivered the shares.'

Mr. Lupton: 'After the conviction?'

Cheiro: 'That has happened to many a bank before now, I think.'

"Replying to other questions of Mr. Callan, he said that he never made any secret of the fact that he was Cheiro. There was a photograph of him in the memoirs that he published fourteen years ago, and quite recently his photograph was printed in a Sunday paper with a circulation of about a million, in which he published his recollections as Cheiro.

"Countess Mena Le Warner Hamon corroborated her husband's evidence.

"Michael Daly, who said that he was caretaker of the factory, was examined, and stated that on the 15th of August, when he left at 8:20 o'clock to go to Ballycumber, the factory was quiet, and when he got back about 10:30, the place was on fire. He could do nothing to save it. He lived in a hut near the factory and on the 1st of April 1923, when he was in bed, there was a tap at the door, and a voice asked if anyone was there. He said yes, and the voice told him that the peat turf was all on fire, that the hut was in danger, and that he would want to look out, but that if he stirred within a half-hour, it would be at his own risk. He waited for half an hour and then went out.

"Compensation was not granted in view of the fact that the factory had not been restarted and there seemed little likelihood of a resumption of its activities. Certainly no material official encouragement warranted it...."

Cheiro stood up well under this grilling, as he had done before on a long ago occasion in the witness box when his opponent had been the redoubtable Marshall Hall, later to become his staunch personal friend. But it left a nasty taste in his mouth and a scar on his memory, particularly as the net profit to him at its close was precisely nil.

Yet it wasn't in his nature to carry a grudge or to be resentful of an injustice. Occasionally he would turn it all over again in his mind and then say with a sigh: "You know Mena I don't know that I am worse than some of these so-called honest traders and professional men. I don't put sand in the sugar or water down commodities. They have an elastic business morality that is very convenient for their consciences. I try and help people as far as my powers permit. I do know that I have comforted and eased the burdens of many troubled souls, so I can't see but that I've been as honest as most, and probably more useful than some."

But enough of the past and dead projects, for now a new vista opened up. This was nothing less than an invitation from Hollywood! Glittering and magnificent! Cheiro had always benefited — in health and fortune — in the United States, particularly in sunny California.

Mena had enjoyed a period of residence there as well, in her twenties, and it was her mother's homeland. The New World beckoned, and with great eagerness they turned their faces to the West and embarked on yet another adventure with renewed hope.

Chapter Sixteen

The New World

New Year's Eve 1927, and Mena and Cheiro were again at sea, bound for the United States, but this time with a business objective in mind, as well as to benefit their health from the sunshine and ozone.

Negotiations were in progress with Hollywood film magnates to re-issue, adapt or incorporate a series of films demonstrating Cheiro's *Language of the Hand*. The idea was that by showing the hands of current screen celebrities, indicating their past and probable future, according to the lines of their palms, it might greatly add to the interest in both Cheiro and palmistry. Cheiro had a lot of material available. There were his many books published since the turn of the century, the sale of which greatly added to his income. He was also doing lectures, which audiences everywhere, especially in the United States, found so absorbing. And there were his innumerable consultations. In addition, he had recently made a small film about palmistry in England, which had succeeded far beyond expectations, so it seemed that the demand for films on palmistry by Cheiro undoubtedly existed, and it was only necessary to negotiate the terms. These were expected to be very generous because it all occurred during one of Hollywood's most lavish and fantastic periods.

A year before Cheiro's visit to California, he had made, at his own expense, in London, a series of eight reels teaching and explaining the meaning of the lines in the hand.

These films were called *Cheiro's Language of the Hand*. It was illustrated by black and white drawings, showing the various markings on the hand, with text on the side explaining what each line meant. A pointer was added that moved from line to line as the words changed.

With each example, there appeared on the screen the impression of some famous person's hand, taken from life, autographed and dated. Among those used from Cheiro's personal collection was the hand of Prime Minister William Gladstone, which he had given to Cheiro during an interview at Hawarden Castle about twelve months before he died. Another was Lord Kitchener's, signed by him on War Office stationery and dated July 21, 1894, when Cheiro made the prediction that he would not meet a soldier's death on the battlefield, but would die by drowning caused by shipwreck in his sixty-sixth year.

Other hands used in this series were Joseph, Lord Russell of Killewen, Admiral George Dewey, hero of the Spanish-American War, Sir Edward Marshall Hall, Sarah Bernhardt, Lily Langtry, and other celebrated people. This series also showed the mysterious mark on the hand called the *Line of Success* and samples from life bore out that success could be seen on the hand. From the time indicated on their hand, success came to that person no matter what business they were in or what career they followed!

Before these films were finished, viewers were taught on what part of the hand marriage was indicated, and illustrations were given, showing happy unions, separations, divorces, as well as a hand of a woman who went to the gallows for poisoning her husband in order to marry her lover.

Each film explained one line at a time, and was followed the next week by another, until the whole subject was covered. When Cheiro made this series, he believed they would appeal to the strongest interest in human *Nature*, namely that of self, but neither the exhibitors nor he had estimated the enormous interest these films would have.

The audience that saw the films the first week came to see what subject would be covered the following week. The public's interest increased for the entire eight weeks. At Sir Oswald Stoll's theatre, the Coliseum in London, at the end of the films, people would block the corridors to get under a light to see if their own hand bore a mark they had just seen. In the end, all the lights had to be turned on in the cinemas where the films were shown to prevent people leaving their seats.

The demand for the series was so great that, at one time, over a thousand cinemas in Britain were showing them every night. In addition, more than one hundred thousand copies of one of Cheiro's books, *Read Your Past, Present and Future* were sold during the eight weeks the films ran.

Having proved that the appeal of such films could wake up even a conservative country like England, Cheiro took them to Hollywood with the intention of remaking them and issuing them in the United States.

Within ten days of reaching the film Mecca of America, Cheiro submitted the reels to one of the large film companies, RKO. Within twenty-four hours he got a call from an executive at the firm. Cheiro was told: 'Miss Pickford, Mr.

Fairbanks and myself looked at your series last night. (Mary Pickford — *America's Sweetheart* — Douglas Fairbanks, Sr. and Charlie Chaplin owned RKO in the 1920s and '30s.) We think they are of enormous interest, but all short subjects must be passed by the staff in New York. Will you give us an option while we send them there to get their reply? The principal director here is so enthusiastic about these films that he is writing to New York himself, to recommend them. So you are not running any risk in waiting for the answer from New York.'

Cheiro waited. To the astonishment of everyone concerned, the wise men in the East wrote back that they were full up with short subjects and could not consider the *Language of the Hand* for twelve months.

Then another large film company asked Cheiro to submit the series to their representative in Hollywood. He did so. Again all were enthusiastic, but again the head office in New York had to be consulted. He was asked to delay his departure for England for a month to enable one of the administrators in New York to reach Hollywood. He agreed but the arrival of the man kept being delayed. Time passed, until the week before Cheiro was booked to sail. At last the man arrived in Hollywood but he had to return to New York the next day. Cheiro was told to wait two months for his return.

Cheiro said no and prepared to leave once again for London. Twenty-four hours before he left, he got an offer from a larger film company with terms that were acceptable. The only point he insisted on was that the business be concluded in Hollywood, with no interference from New York. This was agreed, and Cheiro was happy that his film *Language of the Hand* was shortly to be produced on a much larger scale and with greater possibilities than ever.

This is just one example showing the loss of time and money caused by divided control in Hollywood. It has been estimated that this series on the hand, when issued, would represent a turnover of at least a million dollars a year, since the cost of production — being simply camera work — would be extremely small and the profits would be huge and out of all proportion to the usual profit calculations in making pictures. Yet this was jeopardized by this system of dual control which Cheiro called one of the greatest evils in the film industry.

While in Hollywood, Cheiro became fascinated with the customs and background that made it part wonderful dream, composed of beauty and glamour, part stairway to the stars, each step a heartache and a disappointment for the many who would never scale the heights, and part terrifying nightmare, which could not happen anywhere else but in this world of make-believe.

To people coming from more sedate European lifestyles, the bizarre goings-on seemed just too fantastic to be true. But to Cheiro, whose own life had been so incredible, these newcomers to celebrity and riches were just spoiled, wayward children of fortune, to be humored and, perhaps, forgiven their youth and immaturity. For a person accustomed to the *haute monde* of European society in the Victorian and Edwardian eras, the Hollywood aristocracy and claimants to fame seemed crude, bogus and pretentious. The riches came too quickly, which led to extravagant ostentation, thoughtless cruelty and childish generosity, accompanied by lavish wanton spending and waste. Nevertheless the Hamons met many intriguing, entertaining and charismatic personalities and the climate and atmosphere were superb for their health!

These were the days of spectacular, dizzy rises to unassailable positions of fame and fortune. Extravagance of one's conduct and money was condoned; indeed was expected as evidence of possessing genius and artistic temperament.

Different laws of the various states of the union — some liberal, some prudish — no doubt contributed to a certain confusion of outlook. This was the heyday of prohibition, which meant not that ye shall be drinkless, but that ye had better have access to a reliable bootlegger — preferably one with legal backing.

Initially this stranger within the Hollywood gates had difficulty contacting a reliable supplier. Cheiro liked to take a drink whenever the spirit moved him and suffered a sense of aggravated deprivation when he was handed, in restaurants, what at first looked like a wine list but turned out to contain soft drinks under deceptive names. Once, at a house-warming party given by a celebrated star and his wife, he was introduced to an innocent looking concoction known as "*Mother's Milk.*" The result was disastrous! It required the heavy pummeling of a huge, grinning, black female masseuse in his hotel room the next day before he revived; a shaken, sadder, but much wiser man. Even this condition, however, was better than that of some of the other guests; at least a dozen had to be sent to hospital to have their stomachs pumped! The host and hostess telephoned in the morning, full of concern. Their new bootlegger, it seems, had mistakenly sent them embalming fluid — instead of Holland's Gin!

Doctor's orders produced a government certificate that allowed any druggist in Los Angeles to supply eight ounces of government brandy once every two weeks. But not many pharmacists had this medicine of the gods.

"You'd think we were in search of the Holy Grail, from the reaction of some of the drugstore owners we tried," Cheiro observed.

Finally they hired a cab, and after four hours of diligently searching, found a bottle of booze at a cost, Cheiro figured, of twenty dollars, about three dollars an ounce! The Irish Seer said in amazement: "No wonder I kept looking at my eight-ounce bottle!...I didn't dare touch it until I went to bed!"

The bottle was a curiosity in itself. It had government instructions and warnings printed all over it. It had a customs seal on the cork; then a government stamp saying the tax had been paid; next a government certificate that it was pure brandy. Then came a terrible warning: 'If the person to whom this amount of eight ounces is given, should pass this bottle or its contents to any other individual not herein named by the certificate, they will be liable to prosecution.'

And lastly, 'When the bottle is empty, the person to whom it has been issued will be held accountable to destroy the labels on said bottle!'

So, like many other honest men before him, Cheiro became a lawbreaker and began to seek out an honorable bootlegger. Talk about an oxymoron. He owed his introduction to this syrupy-voiced individual, to a friend — a judge — in one of the Courts. The liquor he got was genuine and reasonably priced.

"How do you manage to do it?" Cheiro once asked. "There must be a lot of helpers to pay, boats that run the stuff ashore, or across the border, and all that sort of thing?"

"It is my big turnover," the pleasant voice explained. "Besides, I get large parcels of stuff seized by the prohibition agents at knockdown prices. It wouldn't pay me to try and pass off anything bad on you. I really do try to be an honest bootlegger. If I can't get good stuff, I won't sell any. Many prohibition agents have too much love of good sentiment in every business, and I encourage it in mine...sentiment and a fair share of the profit has carried me through till now."

"Will you join me in a drink?" Cheiro inquired.

"Me? Absolutely not! I never drink. I'd be too afraid of losing my head, and I keep the interests of my wife and six kids in mind at all times. They're downstairs in my car right now, because, you see, federal officers never like to search a man's car with children in it. Most of them are family men themselves, and that's where sentiment comes in again."

Later, when the two men became better acquainted, Cheiro learned more of this man and his plans and learned a side of human life along with a few fragments of philosophy he might never have known if he hadn't become friends with this Hollywood bootlegger. The man was a Polish Jew who was ten years old when he arrived in the United States with his immigrant parents. They became invalids, broken by early privation and persecution. He was the only survivor of their six children. Without money or friends, without knowing the language, his struggle was a hard one. His father died. His mother was paralyzed by a streetcar accident and he became her sole supporter. First he sold newspapers and cleaned shoes for *colored* waiters in a downtown hotel. He wouldn't apply to any Jewish organizations for charity. All he asked for was work. Work came, and money.

Ten years later he had saved enough to bring his mother to Los Angeles, in the hope that she would benefit from its warm climate. Then he bought a small schooner and took fresh fruit from the port of San Pedro to incoming ships: "The God of Abraham looked down upon me, and I prospered," he reflected. This work opened up to him the secrets of the surrounding coast. War threw him into rum running. "Two things Christians will always pay for are food and drink." He built up quite a reputable clientele — stars, judges, bishops, priests and leaders of many of the new religious cults that were a distinguishing feature of the Hollywood scene at the time.

"What are you going to do with all the money you must be making?" queried Cheiro.

"First, I'm trying to have my mother cured; second, I will give my children the best education money can buy; and lastly, I want to buy some land in Palestine where my wife and I can end our days in the land of our forefathers.

What irony. This was another side to the usual picture presented to tourists and residents. The stars glittered, by day and by night, in public and, even more so in private. Every now and then a campaign would get under way to clean up the private lives of celebrities in that spot lit town. Excesses that probably started in rivalry as evidence of artistic temperament and as publicity stunts, or even as a new thrill for those who lived on excitement, would cause reputations to come crashing down. For no sooner was a star firmly established in the ascendant, than he occupied a mansion on the topmost crag of some height within view of the envious ones he was outstepping.

Cheiro was introduced to many of the peculiar offshoots of Hollywood — including the many cults that attracted many devout, fanatical adherents. For instance, he was shown the rites and ceremonies of the *Daughters of Truth* a nudist group that later went into eclipse in spite of all its vows of celibacy and high-toned ritual, because the teacher bolted with all the money while the women members somehow became — pregnant!

Cheiro met the movie greats of the day, at work and at play. He also met ordinary people, the cop on the corner and the drugstore clerk. He was interested in them all and as usual, conquered them with his charm. So often have I heard, even from the *grand dame* of theatre and movies herself, Lillian Gish — whose palms I, too, personally examined— about his power to charm... reducing a chattering mob of society women to purring kittens because "Cheiro was coming to tea," or how he befriended a wayward servant in her hour of need, as she sobbed her gratitude.

When the time came to return to England, it was with the film contract securely in his pocket. He and Mena returned only to pack their goods prior to this final voyage across the sea, to establish themselves permanently in Hollywood.

Alas, "Man proposes..."

Chapter Seventeen

Hollywood!

Getting rid of property, leases, packing up and closing down a twenty-two-servant house in London — all such related matters occupied the next nine months of their lives. Eventually everything was settled, passage was booked on the "Capiciganshire," and off they went.

The group included Cheiro and Mena, her son, Jack, an elderly aunt, Cheiro's valet and chauffeur and their maid. And so, as the sun sets in the West, our intrepid travelers bid a fond adieu to England, as they set out for the New World and — HOLLYWOOD!

In Hollywood they received a royal welcome. Both now and during his former visit to arrange the film contract, Cheiro had declined, with a few exceptions, to read the fortunes of those aspiring to fame who thrust out their hands so anxiously to him. "I have retired," he often joked. "Soon you will be able to pursue the study yourself if you practice the lessons that will be given to you on the silver screen."

He threw himself into getting spacious but reasonably priced accommodations because of the recent setbacks in the Old World, with which he had now severed relationships. He hoped this time he would truly be able to make his headquarters in the United States and establish a permanent home in Hollywood.

They finally decided on a large, rambling house in the old colonial style, set in thickly wooded grounds with spacious rooms. The house was ideal for the considerable amount of entertaining they were expecting to do. The rooms on the ground floor all connected with each other via double sliding doors and for really large parties the rooms could quickly be converted into one vast salon with screened-in porches at each end. This led on to a wide terrace ringed by long, lush, trees that swayed gently in the cool night breeze.

There were ornamental urns from which swung festoons of blossoms. Bright shrubs and creepers flung vivid patches of color here and there. A fountain, much like the famous Trevi fountain in Rome, splashed over fat, contented goldfish, so tame they would eat right out your hands. Flowery pergolas made perfumed, lattice avenues of shade on hot summer days.

Cheiro and Mena received a great diversity of notable personalities, people whose own lives and fabulous success had enabled them to turn mere existence into an exciting life for themselves and their friends; everyone who succeeded in Hollywood in those days lived a life comparable to a twentieth century fairy tale.

For a while, even they got caught up in this tidal wave of glitz and glamour, with its frenzied, hypnotic effect on newcomers with stardust in their eyes. William Randolph Hearst, the multi-billionaire newspaper king, introduced them to his fabulous Spanish-style castle, San Simeon, built on top of a mountain, an estate of two hundred and seventy-five thousand acres on the California coast. This legendary palace of white marble, perched high in the clouds, was surrounded by marble terraces, masses of flowers and priceless statuary. The entrance hall was hung with ancient and costly tapestry that blended in with the oriental carpets and contrasted with the huge carved stone fireplaces. On the grounds, guest houses were tucked away to accommodate his friends.

Each outbuilding was a gem itself, one incorporating an interior brought from the Doge's Palace in Venice. There was also a large private zoo, well stocked with strange and exotic creatures from every wild and far-flung part of the world.

They went to Santa Monica, playground of the stars, where luxury prevailed at the Beach Club and celebrities who had mansions in the vicinity, kept open house. Wild celebrations continued twenty-four hours a day as revelers caroused and partied-on, hour after hour, day in and day out, with guests coming and going from one mansion to another — where an even more wild party would be in full swing! These parties had full orchestras — with musicians in tuxedos — playing inside and outside on the terrace under the sun, the moon and the stars — non-stop!

Everybody was always good-humored and entertaining, mainly because everybody was always drunk and whenever sensational stories went the rounds — which was often — they were related in such a way as to be surprisingly free from malice. It seemed that there was nothing, or almost nothing, too fantastic to be imagined, and if something could be thought up -- it would be done! These stories seemed to build to a climax, each one out-shining the last, until finally one event would overstep that invisible line of credibility and so-called normal public opinion. Then reputations would teeter, and another tightrope walker on the highwire of fame would lose his balance, hesitate, and then sometimes recover.

Such an instance was provided by a very popular star who, following the customary pattern of screen success, built himself a lavish dwelling on the edge of a precipice, so that from this great height he might look down on mere mortals. Here, one evening, he awaited the arrival of his mistress, an equally famous star, renowned for her artistic temperament, immaturity and "unnatural tastes". The pathway was covered with rose leaves and after relieving her of her ermine wrap -- that was the envy of Hollywood -- he regaled her with cocktails served in precious, jeweled-encrusted gold cups looted from Russian royal treasure. They smoked cigarettes through diamond-studded holders, toyed with caviar soup and imported Scottish grouse, toasted their love in champagne laced with absinthe, sipped café and liqueurs, and smoked hashish.

Having dismissed the distasteful topic of the stupid director who that morning had dared to offer suggestions during shooting, they whined and complained to each other, deploring the fact that life provided their delicate sensibilities with too few sensations!

Then the lady, for no apparent reason, suddenly began taunting her host to entertain her better and more originally because, after all, carpets of rose leaves have been done so often and hashish is a poor substitute for the reality of oriental desires.... Wasn't there something he could suggest — anything to mark this night as a milestone in her life?

The celebrated brow furrowed in intense concentration, stung by the look he saw in those glorious, half-hooded eyes across the room. He threw the windows open and leaned over the iron railings of the balcony! Below shone the million lights of Los Angeles; above hung the glittering skies and beyond lay the smooth ocean, a sheet of silver reflecting the calm, impassive moonlight, while beneath him lay a yawning precipice. The night was so bright that the rocks below gleamed up at him like the teeth of sharks waiting for their prey.

The backdrop was perfect! Ah-hah! At last he had it! He ran back into the room and picked up the phone.... There was a night rehearsal at one of the studios and a hundred extras would be there — girls who were the pick of the Hollywood beauties and girls who would be hungry at that hour and who would go anywhere for a free meal — or a drink!

Half an hour later, the grinding noise of shifting gears could be heard climbing up the steep avenue — Fords, Cadillacs, Rolls-Royces and Packards — one after another they reached the villa.

Supper was set for forty, and easily that number of Hollywood beauties were soon making inroads on the food and drinks that would have driven any respectable butler to distraction. Girls who had never tasted absinthe in their lives before — were now introduced to the green dragon. Their good-looking host was graciousness personified. He filled their glasses and the more they drank, the more handsome and debonair he appeared. A fever of wild excitement filled the air and spread from one to the other; there was nothing they wouldn't do for such a generous host. They all claimed to be good sports, ready for anything! Was there something he wanted them to do?

The big star looked over at his lover, still reclining lazily on the divan, expressing no surprise at this invasion, but still with that look of scorn and boredom.

He stepped out on the balcony. The moonlight was whiter than ever, the gardens bright as day. Again he leaned over, observing and studying the precipice beneath, while again, that same devilish expression passed across his face. Two men brought in coils of rope and fastened ends of it to the ironwork above the window and below the balcony. Then he went back into the room and held up his hand for silence. When he spoke, it was not persuasively, just a quiet, matter-of-fact answer to their impassioned request!

"Girls," he began. "You are all good sports. You are the pick of Hollywood. You have the most beautiful figures in the world and you have said you would do anything — whatever I asked. I am going to put your words to the test. I want to prove I have an original mind. I want to outdo Nero and all his old-fashioned Roman feasts. And I want your beautiful limbs to make Venus herself turn green with envy. I want to do what no man has ever done before: to drape my windows with your sylph-like shapes, trail the female form divine from my balcony, as in olden days when they hung their banners on the outer walls."

The lights switched off, and the moon shot through the windows in silver radiance. Not one girl in the half-mad group refused to do his bidding.

Meanwhile down in Hollywood, a telephone rang. It rang by the bedside of one of the principal producers, the man whose company had sunk millions into the star's pictures. Half dressed, with a cold sweat breaking out on his forehead, he jumped into a car that was always kept ready at his door. He drove so fast he almost flew up the steep mountain to the villa. As he approached in the brilliant moonlight, he could see naked women being tied to the ironwork of the windows. Already a girl with a rope round her waist was dangling from the balcony over the yawning abyss and another was about to follow just as the producer rushed in crying, "Stop! For God's sake, stop!"

They stopped. His arrival probably prevented a tragic accident. Some measure of sanity returned to the trembling girls. Nero sulked in a corner, and all the gratitude he received from his goddess on the divan was to be called a fool for not understanding her artistic temperament.

After that little stunt, Bacchanalian revels and other bizarre, erratic behavior — evidences of artistic temperament — were henceforth frowned upon. And where persuasion, legal argument and threat of financial loss did not work, the merciless eye of the camera proved that a succession of late-night orgies, coupled with a completely self-indulgent life-style of debauchery, did nothing to preserve that dewy freshness which the public loves in its favorites and what the movie moguls call good box office, but which really translates into *"MONEY...LOTS AND LOTS OF MONEY!!"*

Trying to fit into this new environment demanded some degree of adaptability, a sound head and a velvet glove to maintain a modicum of moderation and the Hamons had some hopes of accomplishing this. Plus, the gentle weather was of enormous benefit to their health. Cheiro and Mena settled into the pleasant surroundings and found their large house none too big for the continuous stream of visitors. And they were as pleased to see the celebrities come to visit, since Cheiro had always loved the gaiety and energy of fast society.

They made several trips to San Francisco and it was there that they saw the Graf Zeppelin on her history-making trip when she arrived out of the sunset in the summer of 1929. They also made friends in Santa Barbara, where many millionaires moved into their winter homes with their beautiful gardens when Jack Frost held New York and Chicago in an icy grip. From afar they saw the trim yachts in the harbor and in the distance, the beauties of Catalina Island. They attended the Santa Barbara Fiestas when, for several days, the whole town lived again in the atmosphere of the Dons: men paraded in embroidered trousers, short jackets, crimson sashes and black silk sombreros; women wore Spanish gowns, high tortoiseshell combs and lace mantillas. Even the groomed horses arched their necks proudly as if conscious of the splendor of their old Spanish saddles, lavishly embellished with silver.

At night there were fancy dress balls. At one, Cheiro appeared as Christopher Columbus and Mena as Queen Isabella of Spain. The couple dined on a huge patio of a house belonging to one of the original Spanish families. The only lighting was flares and gigantic candles. Over the balcony that surrounded the patio hung a wide variety of richly colored rugs, and diners were serenaded with old Spanish music, now cheery, now passionately sentimental. Even the instruments added their romantic and picturesque appeal...the marimba contributing its plaintive wail, then another dashing, guitar-strumming caballero, singing a passionate love song, so emotionally compelling that it would hush his audience into silence.

Garbed and sequestered in the time-warp period of Spain's greatness, it was difficult to realize that a modern city lay beyond the old Spanish mansion!

On Sunday afternoons in their own home, the Seer and his beautiful Countess held open house for English tea, instead of the usual prohibition era cocktail parties. It became a favorite weekend ritual, and quite often more people came calling on these Sunday afternoons than the house could accommodate. There was a continuous coming and going of people, some quite interesting and many very famous. And by now they needed this diversion, because they soon had to swallow one of the bitterest disappointments of their lives.

They moved in, got the place more or less shipshape, then decided to give a housewarming party — to introduce new and old friends to their little abode and to return some of the generous hospitality they had received. More than two hundred people came, including many famous movie stars. Among them was Paul Bern, the biggest executive at Metro-

Goldwyn-Mayer Studios, and by his side was Jean Harlow — looking ravishing in a black velvet dress that accentuated her trade mark platinum blonde hair and pale beauty.

Paul Bern and Irving Thalburg had signed a contract with Cheiro, who was to write historical scenarios and other short films on the *Language of the Hand* that would feature hands of the most celebrated Hollywood stars. This was the main reason Cheiro and Mena had moved the whole family and all their belongings to California. The year was 1927.

Six months passed and nothing happened.... Everytime he tried to find out what the studio proposed to do, he was put off with evasive answers.

Afternoon English tea slowly graduated to evening hooch, as the party swung into full gear. It was well after midnight, when one party was at its height, that Paul Bern asked to see Cheiro alone in his study. The two men went off together and behind closed doors but with open windows, through which a muffled background of music, laughter and clinking glasses drifted, he dropped the bomb and handed Cheiro a telegram he received from the New York office. It said the contract was void on the grounds that it had been signed with regard to silent films and was nullified, since talking films had now taken their place.

There are no doubts poor Paul Bern did not enjoy delivering Cheiro this bad news. He said he tried his best to talk the big boys in New York into changing their minds, but to no avail....

There was a film war going on at the time. Hundreds of silent stars who had formerly been paid enormous salaries were suddenly out of work — disposed of, just like that, because they couldn't — talk! Many had high-pitched, squeaky voices or thick, European accents. Even actors and actresses with borderline voices were cut because the primitive sound recording equipment, then available, would not reproduce properly their true voice, usually projecting it higher-toned and thinner.

Like cattle, they were put on trains leaving Hollywood and sent back to their own countries, never to be heard from again. The whole movie industry was undergoing a rebirth, with all its attendant labor pains. They were too late to participate in the fortunes of the suddenly gone silent era, and too soon to share in the new dawn, whose tiny light would burgeon into a brilliant epoch and become known as *The Golden Age of Hollywood.*

To say that this unexpected turn of events upset him — is putting it mildly! Certain that the contract was firm and their future secured, Cheiro and Mena severed all their connections in London, gathered their family and belongings together and moved to Hollywood prepared for some strenuous, interesting, profitable years ahead. And they could not endure the thought of returning to long, gloomy English winters and leaving beautiful, sunny California. So there was nothing else to do but to make the best of things, and stay.

"It will have to be Cheiro again," said Louis, with a wry smile. Once more, he entered *the mists,* and once more it was Cheiro to the rescue!

Chapter Eighteen

Rest and Cure in Ecuador

Cheiro was extremely tight-lipped about his affairs — personal, financial and anything else (being a Scorpio, this was his true *Nature*), so that this Hollywood setback was probably more of a calamity than he let on. Mena was incensed at the stupidity of the studio's decision, and realizing the emotional, physical and nervous strain which his profession imposed on Cheiro, understood his driving wish to be Count Hamon rather than have to make his living, however successfully, as Cheiro.

At the time, it was thought the blow was more to his pride than to his pocket. Which is to say, no one fully appreciated that this was a major reverse in his fortunes, from which he would never really recover, although there always seemed to be plenty of money — especially when he got back into harness as Cheiro and his fees climbed in tune with Hollywood's fantastic standards. On the surface they lived very well and continued to entertain largely and lavishly.

They had the best of cars and the most luxurious accommodations when they traveled. Her son Jack's ability as a pianist brought them in touch with celebrated names in the musical world. They would go to an artistic performance in the famous Hollywood Bowl and, when such singers as John McCormick became familiar friends, they would wander — singing — in and out of the rooms and on the terrace at evening parties in their home.

1933 started badly. Everything went wrong. Cheiro was giving talks on radio as well as many lectures, in addition to his consultations. Exhausted, he suffered a heart attack. Other complications set in and the Seer lapsed into a coma that lasted for three days and nights. It was only due to the great skill of Dr. Charles Bennett that he recovered at all.

Mena spent most of her time between the laboratory and the sickroom. Ever since the First World War she had been interested in the preservation of food, remembering how everyone suffered from lack of many things during that period. Branches of chemistry and entomology had fascinated her all her life and nothing gave her greater pleasure than testing her theories, a few of which achieved quite a spectacular, if limited, success.

Cheiro always sympathized with her predilection for a laboratory atmosphere and she deeply appreciated his encouragement in her experiments. When he became seriously ill in 1933 she was able to put her experience to practical use for his benefit by preparing special food in her laboratory for him, as he was suffering from an endocrine breakdown and a deficiency of vitamins.

Then in early March she went off in the car to do some shopping when suddenly the car seemed to spin round in the road. She called to the driver to turn off the gas and stop the car! Plate glass windows were falling from high buildings — smashing onto the street as other cars on the road also came to a screeching halt — skidding all over the road — crashing into each other! Palm trees lining the boulevard swayed back and forth and masonry came tumbling down like rain! It was a severe earthquake and when things quieted down a little, Mena told the driver to hurry home by the shortest, safest route.

The house at first glance still looked the same and she rushed upstairs to Cheiro's bedroom and found his secretary and the maids stacking up books that had fallen off the shelves — on top of him. The tremor threw him out of bed while he slept! They helped him into Mena's room and made him comfortable. Fortunately, he was only shaken and not seriously hurt. Later, the doctor gave him a sleeping pill and he passed a peaceful night, but Mena stayed up all night listening to the radio announcements telling of widespread ruin caused by the earthquake. Frightening tremors could still be felt for hours.

After a few weeks, Cheiro was able to get up and around again, so they took several pleasant drives to expedite his convalescence. On one of these occasions, they set off by the coast highway to Ventura, then turned inland to Lebec before going on through Arvin and dropping down from the Ridge, stopping to admire a vast marvelous blue lake that stretched below them that proved to be acre upon acre of lupins. The hillsides, too, were splashed by *Nature's* paintbrush with many hued flowers and this unforgettable scene justified California's boast of being the world's largest natural garden.

Antelope Valley was ablaze with California poppies. Spring had turned the generally arid Mojave Desert into a bower of flowers studded with yucca, cacti and Joshua trees, carpeted with evening primroses, sand verbena and desert lilies.

They pulled up to an isolated little dwelling in one of these beautiful spots one night which was run by a Lancashire man. They found out that an unexpected fellow guest was a world-famous violinist. He played through the night while they sat in the adjoining screened balcony, gazing at the magical moonlit hills and valleys and listening entranced to his music. They never saw the musician but found out who he was through discreet inquiries the next morning, after he left at dawn. It was Joseph Heifitz.

Dr. Bennett forbade Cheiro from doing any work and suggested that it would be good if Mena could take him away for a voyage so that his clients could not reach him. He was too tenderhearted not to see people who were in trouble and wanted his advice.

An opportunity came up for them to visit Ecuador, which they took. As they approached Cap San Lucas on their return trip and it became cooler, they collected their things and started packing because they were now near the end their expedition. Mena had taken Cheiro away an invalid and brought him back renewed. Their first visitor was the doctor, who regarded his patient — laughing and sun-bronzed — with amazement. "Marvelous!" was all he could say.

Chapter Nineteen

The Shape of Things to Come

In 1927 Cheiro published his *World Predictions*. The main headings covered the *Fate* of Europe — including Great Britain and the United States, the coming World War, the Restoration of the Jews, the next War of Wars called Armageddon, the promise of Universal Peace and the Aquarian Age.

Publishers who for years had accepted without question any work from Cheiro, shook their heads doubtfully over the content of this book. "Your prophecies are too sensational and the statements are too definite about people in high places," they said.

"Think how you — and we — will look if these things don't happen," they insisted. "Nearly everything you've predicted seems bad! People don't like doom and gloom. Can't you water it down a bit?"

In deference to a potentially nervous public and the publisher's requirements to be more cautious and less definite about people in high places, Cheiro relented. And as we now know, people needed some encouragement for the terrible two decades that were to follow.

Let us hope that this twice in a generation baptism of fire has made men stronger, and will inure them to what appears to be a future prospect of blood and tears. Now we can start to assess the probability of Cheiro's prophecies for the future by the remarkable accuracy with which his predictions for the intervening years have come to pass!

During his declining years, and in the long periods of physical inactivity to which his illnesses condemned him, his agile mind was busy sorting out future impressions granted to his uncanny insight.

As if he was thinking aloud, he would often comment on these visions, following current political, geographical and geological trends and assess consciously, the feasibility of the revelations of the unconscious, intuitive self.

He always meant to extend and simplify his *World Predictions* and his notes indicated the lines along which he intended to do so. Some have already come true, and in others, which are startling enough, there can now be seen the faint stirrings of fulfillment.

What, then, is in store for us?

First let's examine the things which, when he wrote them, seemed so utterly unlikely to happen!

One of the most astounding predictions — at least to readers in England, was that Edward VIII, then Prince of Wales, would never become King.... "He will renounce his throne for the love of a woman, when the *grande passion* enters his life."

Cheiro predicted WWII with its global scope and warned Mena not to go to Europe after 1940! Unfortunately financial constraints forced her to disobey, but she never forgot the warning: He said, "Great Britain shall suffer mightily from prolonged warfare.... London, and other big cities, will be damaged — nearly destroyed!!"

He foretold what then seemed hardly credible, that "the trickle of Jews returning to Palestine will turn into a tidal wave and the world will recognize a new Jewish state there!"

He talked of Italy annexing African territory (Libya); of Britain relinquishing her hold on India and of the religious wars between the Mohammedans and followers of Buddha, that would tear that country apart.

These are some of the things that Cheiro saw in 1925, which have since proved all too true! He also prophesied: "Terrible civil war between Northern and Southern Ireland, inflicting widespread damage against cities like Liverpool, Manchester, Birmingham and the west of England."

For England he saw the slow collapse of her great empire, exacerbated by indecision and apathy among her sons and daughters.

During George V's reign, he accurately predicted that: "Britain will see three crowned heads on her throne within twenty-five years," This was later amplified with a prophecy that King George VI, to whom he referred to as the Duke of York, would suffer in his lower limbs from deficient circulation and before long would abdicate for health reasons in favor of his daughter." He didn't abdicate, but he did die in office, replaced by his daughter Elizabeth II. It wasn't clear if her son, Prince Charles, would succeed her. He raised the possibility that England and France might be joined by closer ties when a "prince of the isles would unite the flags of the lily and the lion under one rule!"

This was only likely to happen after a severe onslaught on Britain by a foreign power!

"The year 1952 will be a *Fateful* one for Queen Mary," predicted the seer. That's the year King George VI died, as did Queen Mary.

According to Cheiro, the coming Aquarian Age would be preceded by strife, upheaval, revolution, floods, earthquakes, plague, carnage and change. "One of these great cataclysmic periods is fast approaching — the kind from which new eras and civilizations are born! Such as are commemorated in legendary history, long before any printed word appears, by the widely separated village storytellers from the many parts of the world, who always survive to tell such epochal tales as the Biblical Flood, Noah and the Ark.

"Expect great and widespread climatic changes and tremendous eruptions from many new volcanoes - particularly from those hitherto believed long extinct! Premonitory tremors of great earthquakes to come have already caused a rise in the floor of the Atlantic Ocean and alarm among those interested in trans-ocean and coastal business. The Azores will rise as the lost continent of Atlantis is rediscovered.

"This rise in the ocean's bed will create a deflection in the course of the Gulf Stream, making parts of the Arctic much warmer, but rendering northern and mid-Europe - including Britain, Scandinavia, the Low Countries, northern France, Germany and Russia -- so cold as to be uninhabitable!

"Mediterranean countries, even the Sahara regions of Africa and India, will grow more temperate and attract a corresponding influx of mass immigration from these newly frigid lands, to more beneficent climes.

"Those already dwelling there will protest, but they will be overwhelmed by the sheer numbers of peoples converging on the land. In particular, Palestine, already partially developed by her new-found Jewish citizens, will blossom as the rose and become an important world granary and industrial centre. Immense new mineral deposits representing untold wealth will be discovered there. The Russian Bear, frozen out of his northern lair, will survey this *Land of Promise* with envious eyes and swoop down, being already several steps nearer the goal of domination.

"This will at first be effected by erosive tactics, eating away a little here, a little there, by infiltration from within, weakening national resistance and powers of perception and discrimination, but later by direct attack over already subdued territory.

"This, then, is the great conflict of Armageddon!!! First it will scatter and destroy ancient cities, cultures...later, it will afflict the New World, eventually centering in Palestine between 1999 and 2027."

Cheiro stopped short of enumerating the fantastic and powerful weapons and the enormous number of casualties in this awful Armageddon, which will ebb and flow, but will wear itself out by about AD 2150. Then a new millenium of one thousand years of peace, plenty and wisely administered justice will begin.

"Although, for a time, Russia may triumph, her ambitions eventually will be overcome. This will be brought about by a wise Jewish leader who will rise up in their hour of bitter need and will guide the whole world towards a new conception of human brotherhood.

"China will long be ravaged by Communist dissension which spreads in a different form to Japan. Subversive elements in many parts of South America will also make trouble, but these are counterbalanced by the severe earthquakes, storms and floods experienced in many lands, especially in this continent.

"Shocked into maturity, the United States will take a responsible but more humble role in world direction, which is then shared in Palestine by Jews, British, Canadians, Americans — and all who helped the Jewish race in her centuries of affliction."

Cheiro himself was not Jewish and neither specifically pro nor anti-Jewish, having had, he said, "both good and bad experiences" in dealing with Jews. But he made this prediction of a glorious fulfillment of their *Destiny*.

"A great new era will dawn for America and for Britain, but each nation has still many hard lessons to learn. America, a victim of her own youth and opulence, has yet to learn humility and discriminating judgment without losing the boyish fearlessness and love of adventure for adventure's sake, which are such lovable national characteristics.

"Britain, old, inbred, inhibited, once wise and balanced in the humanity and resourceful ingenuity of her skilled craftsmen, has rejected the lessons offered by two wars. Presently recovering from the malaise evoked by the feat of enduring, with a stiff upper lip, two wars— even as victors! — eventually will throw aside the false values that prejudice her efforts and encumber her will power.

"With a change of heart, and a return to wise simplicity and hard living, but also its necessary corollary of inner well-being and high thinking, her ancient standards of proud independence and toleration will reappear in her people, however far flung, and they will not fear to live more fully in the worship of God and the love and service of their fellow men.

"France's outlook is not happy. Her star is retrogressive. Her stable elements, alarmed at turbulent, destructive Communist thought and its constant threat of translation into violent action, will, step by step, retreat. Abroad and among her conservative peasantry, each will jealously guard their own prestige and property. Anxiety to preserve the glories of the past is so great, that everything will be sacrificed to maintain style and the old traditions. Men and literature without style leads to the loss of substance and becomes merely ceremony and ritual.

"Germany may yet become England's ally when the dogs of war are again unleashed, if the pathological resentment induced by losing two wars can be overcome.

"Italy will be affected geographically by the climate changes. A sharpening of her already acute land hunger will in turn affect the political scene, and, the importance of Rome will become intensified in men's minds as religious revivals spurt up when disasters strike."

Cheiro was always greatly interested in the life and prophecies of Nostradamus. To some extent, he identified himself with him and with Dr. John Dee, favorite astrologer of Queen Elizabeth I, as his own experiences and his Indian associations gave him a belief in reincarnation.

Referring to the newer members of the Federation of Nations — newer in a modern historical sense— Australia, New Zealand, Canada, South Africa — Cheiro suggested that they may have to re-orient themselves to the new climatic picture, and pass over as unimportant the problems that currently plague their politicians and at times seem insoluble, to concentrate on broader issues.

Cheiro continues: "Asia has not so much forgotten her ancient heritage, and her revived national energies are for a while destined, mistakenly, to flog the insidious slogan Asia for the Asiatics. However, this feverish and malevolent phase will pass. Much wisdom has come out of the East in past ages. The

East is patient. She will overcome this momentary impatience, though that moment may be long as humans view it.

"One thing is abundantly clear," said Cheiro. "The old day of competitive international trade is fast waning, but it is only by worldwide cataclysms that national rivalry will be eliminated and a brotherhood of mankind be achieved. Much must be lost before more is gained. Mental horizons will at last widen to keep pace with the physical when trans-planetary travel becomes an accomplished fact!

"Amid all these shocks, the role of women strikes an outstanding note: As ever, they respond and rise to the occasion when the impact of adversity is felt on their dear ones. Great strides will be made in the public duties of women and the responsibilities entrusted to them, which will entail a minor revolution in the domestic customs of human society. In this, they will be led by the United States, always a pioneer.

"Women will courageously abandon the reform of detail which has confined their attention for so long, even when they have forced themselves into public office, and strike out boldly in defense and cultivation of those prime elements of the good life and its graces for which women have always longed. Not only for themselves, whatever their color, race or creed, but for their partners and the young lives in their care which, generation after generation, have had to grow up in an ever more bewildering world."

Cheiro also confidently predicted that within a relatively short period, a woman President would occupy the White House in Washington."

Chapter Twenty

The End – or The Beginning?

After returning from a second visit to Ecuador, and although there was again a temporary improvement in Cheiro's health, Mena could no longer delude herself into thinking that rest and change would be of any permanent benefit to him.

He was obliged to spend a good deal of time in bed because he suffered from dropsy, a disease in which fluid collects in body cavities or tissue; usually brought on by heart or kidney failure, as well as his many other maladies. His heart had already been weakened by overstrain and the repeated bouts of pneumonia he suffered, not to mention a serious mistake in diagnosis which delayed correct treatment.

When Cheiro lapsed into a prolonged coma, Mena insisted on another medical opinion. An old friend, Dr. Charles Bennett, quickly summed up the situation: "The man is in a diabetic coma!" he exclaimed indignantly. His condition was grave and called for drastic measures! He asked her permission to administer an enormous injection of insulin. "It may already be too late," he said bluntly. "But it's the only chance of saving his life."

Without hesitating she said, "Go ahead!" Within moments his eyelids quivered and once more life flowed back into that wise old face. Henceforth Mena always made sure that Cheiro received his daily insulin injections and prepared special foods for his diabetic condition. One of the symptoms is that the patient, burning up energy at an alarming rate, is always hungry. Sometimes he can have seven meals a day and still be as thin as a rail.

Meanwhile, business negotiations with Ecuador were still alive and it seemed as though they would turn into a really profitable deal. In addition, Cheiro and Mena acquired a half share in a tuna-fishing schooner, and there were periodical reports to be discussed with the captain, who was the other half owner. Then, more bad luck! Mena's son, Jack, who returned as musically brilliant as ever but also as erratic, got severe head injuries when a gigantic hoarding fell on him. At first he seemed to recover, but soon they were forced to admit that something was wrong, and for his own safety he temporarily entered a mental home for treatment.

Mena dared not stop to think what would be the outcome of all these troubles crowding in on her. She went through the days putting on a cheerful face for Cheiro, preparing his food, seeing that he was comfortable and as pleasantly occupied as circumstances permitted, consulting with the captain and the doctors and nurses, keeping an eye on his aunt who was living with them, and from time to time driving over to see how her son Jack was progressing.

She always had to be on hand to administer the injections punctually, and Cheiro had become so dependant on her company that she even telephoned him from the home when she went to see Jack, so that she could be sure he was alright and that he might not think himself abandoned.

Cheiro's long illness and then her son's trouble created a great strain on their bank account. Serious money problems began to loom. Since the day the Hollywood contract was cancelled, Mena had supplemented the family budget from her own capital. Cheiro, who was very proud, did not like this. Indeed, as soon as his consultations were re-established, it did not continue. So great was the demand for his services that hundreds each day had to be turned away. To discourage callers, fees were raised — then raised again — but not even a hundred dollars for a half-hour's consultation dismayed the eager throng. And this was at a time when some people were earning just a dollar a day.

Hollywood's famous continued to pass though Cheiro's threshold and make their way to the Count's study, some with a metaphorical flourish of trumpets, others taking great precautions to make their visits secret. Many a dollar of large amount would drop from the fingers of one famous foreign star into the big brass bowl, kept for donations to charity, whenever she would stop in now and then for conversation practice, trying to perfect her English for new roles in talking films. Was it Marlene Dietrich or Greta Garbo, or both? One of Cheiro's chief attractions was a particularly agreeable speaking voice and manner, which retained just the faintest trace of the warmth of an Irish brogue, although he didn't like being reminded of it.

One evening, while Cheiro and Mena were at dinner, a servant brought a closed envelope. Cheiro opened it, and excused himself to his friends. He was rather pensive when he rejoined them again much later in the drawing room and a name, then very celebrated in the film world, appeared in

174

Cheiro's autograph book with a heartfelt sentence scrawled above it: "To Cheiro, who told me I must go on, and helped me to do it."

Ramon Novarro, the eldest of a large brood of a widowed mother, and a devout Roman Catholic, had hoped to become a priest, but his good looks and charm singled him out for the silver screen and his large earnings helped him relieve his mother's hardships and educate his young brothers and sisters. But the Hollywood life he led went against his grain, particularly the romantic lover roles for which directors and the public thought he was so well suited. With each new part the old inner conflict would be renewed, until at last, beside himself, he came, quietly at night, giving no name, to beg Cheiro's advice.

The mystic looked at this man, who had a vocation for a religious life. Who knows what thoughts passed through his mind. For Cheiro himself had once felt the stirrings of such a call in his youth when, before his father's financial crash, he had been training to take holy orders as an Anglican priest. Maybe he told his visitor of his own early renunciation and something of what life had given him instead.

This man who entered, outwardly the darling of dream matters, the idol of thousands of love-struck girlish hearts, was actually at the end of his rope by reason of his inner strife. But he went away strengthened and steadied by the advice to continue his screen work until his youngest brother and sister got a good start in life, and then to follow his heart's dictates. He took the advice and for awhile became a member of a monastic order. A homosexual, Novarro was murdered at his home in the late 1960s by two male prostitutes. His body was discovered with a rope around his neck, tied to his ankles, and he strangled to death as they tortured him.

One particular evening, while Cheiro and Mena were strolling in their garden, a well-dressed but rather disheveled man made his way abruptly towards them down one of the paths. Without mincing words, he held out his hands — palms upward — and said that he had just robbed a bank!

"I had to do it! There were good reasons. I have my plans all laid out — for my business — and for my escape!" He indicated a nearby waiting car, its engine still running. "As soon as I have succeeded in my objective I'll return this money that I've temporarily 'borrowed'. But I have to have it now! And there was no other way to get it. It's vital! Tell me — will it work? Is it success or failure you see here?"

Cheiro regarded him silently. Mena stood watching them both. "There has been no violence?" Cheiro asked, but it was more a statement than a question.

"None," replied the man eagerly. "Only the threat of it, of course," he gestured apologetically towards his hip pocket...He had the appearance more of a bank clerk than a bank robber.

Mena looked around. She thought she smelled a strange odor. The visitor glanced about him restlessly. There was no one in sight.

"They'll be after me soon — but you can say I haven't been in the house. That's why I came this way," he said, rapidly. "— I've soaked the car with peppermint to put the dogs off!"

In spite of himself, Cheiro's lips twitched, on the verge of laughter.

"Well," repeated the man. "Which is it to be?"

Cheiro took another look at the strong, willful, agitated face and gave the hands a keen scrutiny, replying in one clipped word: "Success."

"Thanks," and, in the same breath of relief, the man was in the car and away. It was quite a while before the police and the dogs reached the house. Men and dogs alike were puzzled, sniffing this strange, confusing trail; no violence, and a clean pair of heels. Cheiro told them the truth, but not the whole truth, and did not give the man away.

It was at a Central American port, during one of their Ecuador trips, that they were sitting one evening in a café when Cheiro notice someone staring fixedly at him.

"You don't remember me?" he smiled. "But you've not changed much — in spite of the white hair!" (His hair had turned white overnight during one of his illnesses.) "Yet, if I mentioned another summer evening in your garden in Hollywood?" he continued, with a knowing smile, "and an unexpected visitor, a man and a car drenched in peppermint?"

"The bank robber!" they both exclaimed.

"Yes, you would have to say that," he grinned ruefully. "But it's true no longer! I did just as I said I would, and paid it all back — with interest."

"Then — you were successful?" Cheiro asked quietly.

He waved his hand towards a prosperous looking business across the street. "Everything worked like a charm. I had it all planned out, down to the last detail, but at the last moment, before escaping, I hesitated. Your one word sent me confidently on my way again. I don't know what I'd have done if I'd been captured. I was desperate. But from then on, I have never looked back. Tell me, did you really see success written in my hand, or only a desperate man with a gun in his pocket, who had just committed a crime?"

Cheiro smiled inscrutably and made no reply....

It was these and many other reminiscences that cheered her sad heart in the brief intervals of that crowded time, as 1936 crept along.

Real Life Stories appeared in 1934 and *Mysteries and Romances of the World's Greatest Occultists* in 1935 and still Cheiro continued, writing, writing. He worked incessantly for months to finish his last book, *You and Your Star*, published just three months before he died. And all the time he was assembling material and notes for a new set of *World Predictions* that he hoped to complete when he recovered. Many of the prophecies he then made verbally have since been fulfilled.

He asked for a big world map to be fixed on the wall at the foot of his bed, and he would lie there gazing at it, or sit up touching — now this country, now that, with a long pointer, as he suggested the trends of world events. And a pretty ghastly picture it looked for the next fifteen or twenty years. Cheiro was upset with the prospects ahead for mankind and by the way his premonitions were being dismissed by his publishers: "I have tried to warn them — and help them — but they won't listen!"

To distract him, Mena welcomed the constant procession of visitors, some friends, others still wishing to consult Cheiro. He was a good patient, although naturally he chafed a little at the increasing restrictions imposed on him. For a long time he continued to protest that he would soon be well again — when spring came — when he could get away for a voyage — and so on.

But it would never be. Passage was booked to Jamaica on the *SS America* for the following October. But now increasing weakness forced him first to dine upstairs, then to keep wholly to his bed. Cheiro was then moved into Mena's room during the day for a change of scene.

Special meals, injections, her son Jack, Cheiro's aged aunt, servants, doctors, nurses, the boat, Ecuador, the laboratory, -- the interminable merry-go-round went on. The doctors advised draining off some of Cheiro's fluid to relieve his dropsy. He consented to this only if Mena could be present to give him moral support.

The doctor shook his head: "She is already undergoing a great strain."

"It's all right, I'll stay with you," said Mena.

"Lift me up, Mena...let me see my last setting sun," Cheiro said. "We all have to come to it.... I have known for some months now that my span of years is coming to a close. You remember, in my hand, it said that I was to die by water? You see it was not at sea after all. This dropsy is slowly drowning me, and when it reaches my heart..."

Now he would lie for long periods motionless, sometimes comatose, sometimes dreaming, half awake, half asleep: "Oh, I've just had such a wonderful experience!" he once told the nurse, after waking up unexpectedly refreshed. "I've been with my guru, my old teacher in India." Mena tried to persuade him to loosen his grip on his business affairs, which he had always clung to so tightly and secretly. "Why do you want to know about all those things?" he asked.

"It's only to help you," she replied.

"You are quite right, Mena," he said suddenly. "I will write down all the names and addresses for you and tell you where everything is to be found. I am sorry, Mena. I'm afraid there will not be a great deal left for you. It seems a poor return for all your years of devotion and all the money you have spent on me too."

"Don't worry," she replied. "You are all I have ever wanted, and we have had so many happy years together. I would like many more, but...." She caught herself just in time.

"Life won't be very easy for you," he continued — warning Mena about Europe, and about the *Fate* of her son. He counseled her to marry again if she found someone she really liked, and made her promise never to try to get in touch with him through séances and spiritualism. "If it is possible, through dreams or in any other way, I will come to you directly, not through others," he promised.

Mena's own resources were dwindling, for much of her once considerable fortune had been expended on the care of Jack, and in seeing that Cheiro lacked for nothing during his last illness. The setting was, as he desired, one of opulence, as he lay there in that great gilded bed which had a regal history, surrounded by smiling faces, willing hands and masses of flowers.

It cost much in time, effort and money to achieve this serenity which enwrapped him and greeted his many visitors, yet she felt it was a sacrifice well worth making, for it spared him the ignominy of the sordid ends that had been the *Fate* of most of his illustrious predecessors in mysticism and astrology — Dr. John Dee, Cagilestro, and others. Mena cared little for a wealthy future when faced with the realization of years of loneliness and emptiness without her life's companion.

And even with all the heavy responsibilities – physical, emotional and mental that were heaped upon her, she somehow wished his life could be prolonged indefinitely.

When the end came, it still seemed sudden to her, although she had long been expecting it and knew it was inevitable.

Cheiro whispered some numbers to her: one and five. As a person born on the first of the month, he was fortunate in having four numbers that were particularly propitious for him: one, four, two and seven. The first of October went by, then the fourth. With great difficulty, he survived the seventh.

In his death as in his life, strange manifestations crowded in on Cheiro as his passing drew near...up and down the corridors and the stairs, unseen hosts paraded. The room where he lay dying became terribly cold, despite a high temperature elsewhere. His dog shivered and begged to go in to him, although its hair stood on end. Knocks sounded, doorbells and telephones rang -- yet no one, or no visible human, appeared or spoke. Outside, the owls kept up a dismal hooting.

These manifestations were witnessed not only by Mena but also by Edith Phelan, his plain-spoken and experienced English nurse and by Frances Kernan, a student of the Seer, and an authority on astrology.

As one o'clock approached, an overpowering perfume of roses and lilies of the valley pervaded the darkened room in which Cheiro's face stood out strangely luminous, like an alabaster lamp lit from within. Yet there were no flowers in the house.

Then, at 1:05 AM, on October 8, 1936, three weeks before his seventieth birthday, his weak pulse slackened, the tired heart stopped beating and Cheiro passed into the *Great Beyond*. Mena closed his eyes and made the sign of the cross on his forehead.

Three times during the day, that hall clock gave its own warning. It struck one, no matter what the hour. Then, at his death, it stopped forever and never worked again.

Not long after, Mena found a single red flower on the counterpane at his feet. But by whom? And from where? There were no such flowers then blooming in the garden, and no others besides Mena and the nurse had entered the room.

Cheiro was dead.

At first Mena was conscious only of numbness and the sense of released tension from years of care giving. The taut readiness was no longer required. Overtired, *Nature* asserted herself. Mena's vocal chords refused to function and she lost the power of speech for three days. Sedatives were administered and she was prostrate with nervous exhaustion.

Her son Jack's first knowledge of his stepfather's passing came with an announcement over the radio. It shocked him into reasonabless and he clamored to be allowed to come home to be by his mother's side. Sympathetic friends, especially Mrs. Kernan, carried out Mena's wishes with regard to the last rites. A death mask was taken and a cast was made of his hands, once so firm and shapely, now twisted and drawn, that had comforted and reassured thousands of others.

The boulevards and the grounds of the house were thronged by curious sightseers and souvenir hunters. The house was full of newspapermen. Telegrams and cables arrived from all over the world, followed by thousands of letters.

For years missives from strange places and curious people continued to arrive. There was much coming and going, but Cheiro's dog never left Mena's bedside, not even to eat or drink. He put his nose in her hand, looked at her with tragic eyes and, with a pathetic, whimpering sob, licked her fingers. In the past, no one could even approach the house without him barking furiously. This magnificent dog resembled the well-known film star, Rin-Tin-Tin, and was of the same stock. He had been with Cheiro for six years and idolized his master.

Mena left for the funeral parlor with Mrs. Kernan. The car was a mass of flowers that were taken to the room where Cheiro was lying in state. The funeral parlor was dominated by the beautiful polished rosewood casket. It was draped in white velvet and bore a multitude of floral offerings. The open lid was lined with ivory satin and within the casket lay his long, still form, in full formal attire, wearing his decorations and his Masonic orders. His head rested on a satin ivory pillow, his features composed as if not dead, but merely sleeping. All age had slipped away. His hands were loosely folded, and into them Mena placed red roses.

She looked long and hard at her soul mate, but still, tears refused to come. Grief was deep within and it made her into an automaton, carrying out these last duties.

Dr. Bennett was at the house when Mena returned after ordering a seven-pointed star, the *Seal of Solomon*, from the florist. But he was concerned about her continued rigidity and ordered more bromide. Mena ordered that the funeral should take place the next day at 5 o'clock, the hour Cheiro had told her would be so important.

On the day of the funeral, there was a morbid crowd outside the house and the police were requested to guard the house and grounds during the funeral, for fear of souvenir hunters. Thousands of people lined the route.

The funeral service was held in the private chapel. The Masonic service began, two brother Masons officiating. Cheiro's Masonic apron was held up for all to see and age-old solemn words were repeated. Hundreds were present, and everyone wept as the grand cadences swelled from the organ as the public filed past, beholding for the last time the mortal remains of the *Prophet of The End Times*, a man so dearly beloved. Clutching the side of the casket, Mena collapsed...

Weeks of sorting out papers and packing followed the funeral. Only now did Mena learn that her circumstances would be greatly reduced. She could no longer afford to remain in the large house where they had dwelt so happily for the last few years

There were also debts to be settled, for in his anxiety over money, after having been accustomed for years to having so much, Cheiro had, unknown to Mena, borrowed on all sides. It was then she discovered that the two principal sources of his income ceased with him. They were annuities from France paid for by aristocrats for whom he had performed great services in the past, before their marriage. And as a bachelor, without family ties, he had not troubled with life insurance and then, around the time of his marriage, insurance companies refused to sell him a policy because of his health.

Then there was the auction and removal of household objects, the settlement of accounts, and a last walk through the gardens. And finally, the painful parting with Cheiro's pet dog, Lupe.

Mena left their house for the last time after visiting each room and pausing for a brief prayer in Cheiro's room. On July 30, they were scheduled to sail for Jamaica on October 17, and now, three months later, Mena sailed alone, occupying the same suite they had booked but instead of Cheiro being with her, the bed that should have been his was the resting place for the valise which contained the bronze urn that held his ashes, and in his hat box was his death mask and a cast of his right hand.

Mena said farewell to the servants and made the thirty-mile drive to San Pedro Harbor. She went on board the SS *America* and listlessly watched the four tons of baggage being loaded. Farewells followed as the ship slowly moved away from the dock.

Like someone in a trance, she watched the shores of California slip away, the snow on Mount Bauldy, and the line of the Sierra Madre grow fainter and fainter. A whale spouted in the distance. Someone came and took her down to her cabin, and when the stewardess arrived, she found that Mena had fainted. She was put to bed and remained there for two days. On the evening of the third day she stood at the window of her cabin and watched the sun drop into the Pacific Ocean like a ball of fire.

The last time she did this, her life partner was with her, and together they had watched the gorgeous sunset on this same route. Now everything was changed. And then, though she had not wept before, she felt tears run down her face and splash on her breast like hot rain. Never, in all her life, had she wept as she did then. The flood gates finally let loose...

Much later, when everyone else had gone to bed, Mena crept on deck and remained there all night, watching the sea, the stars and at last, the dawn, praying for God to comfort her and to give her courage. As she gazed out over the peaceful ocean, Tennyson's words ran through her mind:

Kind hearts are more than coronets,
And simple faith more than Norman blood.

Cheiro possessed both.

The End

ANTHONY CARR's Accurately fulfilled predictions!

New York
"A great disaster will strike a major city creating a yawning chasm as earth and buildings topple into eternity. There will be a terrible plane crash over New York City. Watch for a sign in the heavens that will shock the whole world! It will be like a bolt of lightning – and put the fear of God into us." (Documented on January 1, 2001 and August 14, 2001)

Washington
"I see raging fires around the White House in Washington D.C.! Sabotage in D.C. – black smoke and fire!" (Prophesied and documented January 1, 2001)

US Politics
It won't be long before President-elect George W. Bush plunges the world into war! (Documented January 1, 2001)
Bill Clinton will be elected and re-elected US President.
The surprizing defeat of New York Governor Mario Cuomo.
The assassination attempt on President George Bush in 1991

World Politics
Saddam Hussein will rise and allies will wage war against him.
Russian Prime Minister Mikhail Gorbachev will be overthrown.
A great fire at the Russian White House.
Oscar winning actress Glenda Jackson goes into politics.

Hollywood
Near-fatal heart problems of Arnold Schwarzenegger.
A love child for superstar Sylvester Stallone and a tall blonde.
A bouncing baby boy for Roseanne.
Destruction of Michael Jackson's career due to a sex scandal.
Lisa Marie Presley's divorce from You-Know-Who.
Toronto will become "Hollywood North."
Legendary singer Ben E. King makes a spectacular comeback.
The failure of Whoopie Goldberg's marriage.
Elizabeth Taylor and Richard Burton reunited for a third and last time.

World Events

The Gulf War.

The Falkland Islands War.

The finding of the Titanic.

The Kuwait oil well fires.

The building of the Chunnel between England and France.

The 'murder' of Pope John Paul I.

The attempted assassination of Pope John Paul II.

The murder of Archbishop Oscar Romero of El Salvador.

Moammar Khadafy responsible for the crash of Pan-Am Flight 103 over Scotland.

Construction of a massive space platform.

US Events

Eruption of Mount St. Helens.

Los Angeles Earthquake of January 17, 1994.

McDonald's massacre where a gunman slaughtered 10 people.

Clergyman and demagogue Jim Bakker - destroyed by scandal

Royalty

The marriage of Lady Diana to Prince Charles.

Princess Diana's bizarre sex scandal and her divorce.

The death of Princess Diana.

Sports

The Toronto Blue Jays will be World Champions for 3 consecutive years.

Carl Lewis "unexpected" Olympic win over Ben Johnson.

The Minnesota Twins come out of nowhere to win the 1991 World Series.

Mike Tyson's boxing career would come to a disgraceful end.

Health

Major breakthrough in heart transplants.

First mechanical heart for Barney Clark.

Discovery of a new drug that allows all organ transplants.

Incredible new 'cocktail' drug for AIDS.

Deaths

The Queen Mother, Princess Margaret, Princess Diana, Elvis Presley, Burt Lancaster, Jessica Tandy, Dean Martin, George Burns, Gene Kelly, Richard Burton, Liberace and Leonid Brezhnev among many others.